COUNTERATTACK

COUNTERATTACK

BEATING FOOTBALL'S ATTACK DEFENSES

by Michael Koehler

PARKER PUBLISHING COMPANY, INC.
West Nyack, New York

© 1986 by

PARKER PUBLISHING COMPANY, INC.

West Nyack, N.Y.

Library of Congress Cataloging-in-Publication Data

Koehler, Mike.
    Counterattack: beating football's attack defenses.

    Includes index.
    1. Football—Offense.   2. Football—Coaching.
I. Title.
GV951.8.K628   1986   796.332'2   86-773

ISBN 0-13-183575-0

Printed in the United States of America

DEDICATION

To two of the Northwood's finest, whose love of the game of football spans generations. To Bud Sexmith, who finds joy in watching, and to Cully Akey, who finds joy in playing—both with unborn memories.

And to my wife, Pat, and to my daughters, Kathleen, Carrie, and Peggy, who bring much love into my life.

INTRODUCTION

Let's admit it. The growth of attack defenses within the past several years has made life a lot more exciting—and a bit more frustrating—for offensive football coaches. The predictability of traditional defensive sets, although never a *sure* bet, provided the offense with several good game-day "guesstimates" of what the opponent was up to. Offensive coaches might expect to run into stunting linemen or an occasional scraping linebacker, sometimes even a safety blitz, but the stunts usually were predictable. Like most coaches, the guys in charge of the defense were reluctant to gamble.

Well, with the advent of offenses such as the triple option, the Houston Veer, and the increased and more refined use of misdirection, it didn't take long for defensive coaches to learn that their predictability was killing them. They decided to get in on the act. If unpredictability was so important for the offense, it ought to be just as helpful to the defense. They decided to attack—from every angle and from a variety of sets.

It was a great idea. No longer sentenced to stand toe-to-toe with a double team block or a tackle trap, defenses started flexing tackles and slanting line charges. The result was confusion for blocking assignments and for the sequencing of plays. And the defensive players loved it. Rather than protect an area, they *attacked* an area. It represented a new and exciting variation on an old and increasingly predictable theme.

Now, the proliferation of defenses using flexed tackles, line slants, and scraping linebackers has caused offensive coaches to reassess *their* strategies. Many of us continue to emphasize our basic offenses, to vary our formations in order to spread out the defense, and to hope that one of our kids can break an arm tackle that will spring him into the secondary. Our mind sets won't let us break from the former value of what we've been doing all these years.

However, what we've been doing just doesn't seem to be working anymore. So some of us are rethinking our offensive strategies. *Our* first consideration was to maintain much of what we'd been doing but to identify complementary plays and minor adjustments in our formations that would give us the edge we needed. We didn't want to shock our system and provoke a complete retooling of the offense. That would have had a negative effect on team morale, and it would have involved far more planning than we cared to undertake. So here's what we did. This book will help you do it, too.

First, it will help you understand what the defenses are doing. We do the same things, so chapter one was a natural for us. It identifies the principles of attack defenses and lists strategies and techniques they use to realize them.

Next, it discusses the strategic value of the Wing T attack. The Wing T provides not only flexibility but the "opening whistle" edge on most attack defenses. Attack defenses try to protect eight gaps along the line of scrimmage. The Wing T confronts them with *nine*. The Double Wing confronts them with *ten*—with no tendencies by formation. Just what advantages these formations provide with motion and how you can exploit them is discussed in Chapter 2.

Next, we discuss how to overload a spot along the line of scrimmage. The purpose is to take a page out of Eisenhower's book and establish a breakthrough somewhere along the line. First, we use backs from their home positions and from the wing and slot positions as blockers. You can use our plays or use yours to put a halfback or the fullback on a defensive lineman or to send him through the line on an iso block on one of the linebackers. Then use your quarterback more as a runner.

The *overload principle* also makes greater use of a formation we developed years earlier to attack the split-6. We call it the Pro 4 formation. It can be varied to include a variety of backfield sets.

Simply position one of the backs, generally one of your best blockers, between the offensive guard and tackle. His added blocking at the point of attack will give you a great deal of flexibility, both with your blocking schemes and with the unpredictability of your running attack. It provides, for example, for one of the most deceptive and quickest-hitting counter plays you've ever seen. More will be said about the actual plays later.

Then we discuss several running plays as they relate to the other backfield sets from the "4" formation. When combined with the "lead" blocking from one of the backs and the "follow" action of your quarterback, the "4" set provides for a lot of strength at the point of attack, enough to muscle through most attack defenses. It gets the lead blocker on the linebacker before the linebacker can get to the gap he wants to plug, and it avoids predictability because it provides several misdirection and play-action passes from each set.

Chapter 8 discusses a delay-action sequence that allows the defense to commit to their stunts *before* the ball hits the point of attack. It's a *run-to-daylight* series, and provides several complements and variations.

Chapter 9 presents several plays that allow you to react off the noseman's stunts; to adjust your line blocking schemes; to make sure your play-action passes complement the adjustments; and to redesign your use of motion to confuse secondary coverage and to sneak a blocker into the point of attack.

An effective format for scouting yourself as well as your opponents is presented in Chapter 12. Like all defenses, attack defenses rely heavily on offensive tendencies. You'll want to chart your tendencies in order to break them every time you play a big game. This chapter is critical for all football programs. Finally, Notre Dame and Wisconsin provide valuable strategic information in Chapter 13.

One of the primary advantages of this book is that it provokes a lot of offensive soul-searching. If you're currently winning football games against attack defenses, you will still pick up added strategies from this book. If, on the other hand, one or more of your opponents is stopping your running game by attacking from a variety of angles and defensive sets, you need new ideas. Attack defenses are sophisticated, well sequenced, and well coached.

To expect to beat them without making necessary offensive adjustments can result in a whole lot of frustration. You can avoid the frustration by taking a good, hard look at what you're doing and by incorporating one or more of the proven strategies that are outlined in this book. The result will be a refined offense that retains everything you like to do but that provides the adjustments needed to counter the attack.

CONTENTS

1

Identifying the Enemy: What Attack Defenses Try to Do

Attack defenses have provided new dimensions to the planning activities of offensive coaches. The changes have been refreshing. As a matter of fact, most of the offensive coaches I know have welcomed the challenge. The "Make Something Happen" battle cry of the attack defense has introduced an unpredictability that has all of us on our toes. When we're on our toes, we're not dragging our feet.

We *have* to be on our toes, or the maze of bodies hurling themselves at us will bury us. And "bury" is exactly what they're doing to some offenses. The principle underlying the design of most attack defenses is "Don't defend—Attack!" The offense that is unwilling or unable to adjust is in a lot of trouble.

Coaches will find themselves unable to sequence their plays properly. Line blocking assignments will become hopelessly confused; backfield execution will be cut short due to defensive penetration; and, most important, players' confidence in their own ability and in the wisdom of their coaches will be lost somewhere on the practice field.

"Get out there and play football!" doesn't work anymore. The old truism that games are won or lost "in the trenches" is as valid as it ever was, but the spoils of trench warfare no longer go just to the strongest. More often than not, they now go to the smartest and the quickest. Even the biggest, strongest linemen block a lot of air if they don't know what to look for and how to react to it.

So let's develop a battle plan, first by getting to know the enemy better. Just what is the average attack defense trying to do, and how is it trying to do it?

CHARGE!

The first thing they're trying to do is jam the line of scrimmage. A fireplug of a noseguard, if he's quick enough, can make a mighty big pile if he can beat the center to the gap inside either guard. A linebacker scraping into the other gap can do the same thing. He can also find a clear path to the ball carrier if the onside guard fails to pick him up. That's why they "charge!" Their purpose is to attack each gap on the line of scrimmage, to penetrate wherever possible, and to confuse the daylights out of the blockers. They usually succeed. Here's how.

Consider the basic 5-2 alignment—or maybe an offset 4-4, so the defense has a noseman. First of all, it's important for us to recognize that attack defenses don't like to sit and slug it out. So we can be sure that the noseman is going to stunt *somewhere*. He may be looping into either gap or slanting into one of the two offensive guards, but he's going to be moving. If we do our homework, we can fashion at least a general idea of where he might be going. Satisfactory predictability is better than nothing.

"Doing our homework" suggests the need for us to scout ourselves in order to maintain a cumulative record of our tendencies by formation. The organization of such a process is discussed in a later chapter. For now, it is important for us to realize just what we are doing from each formation. Combined with the defensive scouting reports of our opponents, we can use that information to either break our tendencies or to entice the opponent into semipredictable defensive adjustments and then modify our blocking schemes to accommodate them.

Figure 1-1 illustrates a 4-4, offset to provide an odd look in the middle. The defense is designed to stop the running attack up the middle. It can do more, but it wants to raise havoc in the middle of the line. The general tactic, as evidenced with the dotted line, is to send the noseman into the gap between the center and the offensive left guard and to scrape the right linebacker in the opposite direction.

We have discovered, for example, that a lot of our opponents like to use the strategy against us because we normally get a lot of mileage out of our fullback with our cross fire series. Figure 1-2 illustrates an "Open T10/Cross fire at 1" with straight blocking. As indicated in the diagram, the play is in a lot of trouble.

Our opponent knows, as we do—at least we *ought* to!—that we run certain plays from the "Open T 10" formation and that one of the

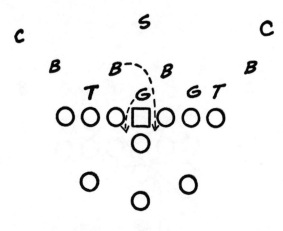

Figure 1-1

favorites is a Cross fire at 1 with the fullback. So he has decided, intelligently it seems, to jam the hole with the noseman and to send the linebacker in the opposite direction to catch the left halfback in the event *he* receives the ball.

It's a good strategy. Ask any proponent of attack defenses. But we can counter the attack by trapping the side of the line to the noseman's slant. First of all, even the most devout advocate of the 4-4 and its many variations will have to admit that it's "trappable." Any play run from our T8 formation that simulates cross fire action and that provides for a quick trap is likely to pick up yardage.

In this case, we'll call a "T8/Crossbuck trap at 3 (also illustrated in figure 1-2). The two-team block on the noseman will neutralize him. The left tackle has a natural angle on the linebacker, and if the linebacker stunts himself out of the play, the tackle can move rapidly upfield to the safety.

Two-teaming the noseman is nothing new. A lot of offenses are "countering the attack" by double-teaming the noseman. But when combined with well-conceived trap plays, particularly those that go against offensive tendencies, the action gives most attack defenses a lot to handle. We've used this play several times within the past few years, and it has resulted in big yardage for the fullback, particularly when we spread out the defense with a split end and a flanker.

It's not a sure thing. There is no such thing as a sure bet when playing an attack defense. Unpredictability is their hallmark. But we can help ourselves out immeasurably if we scout ourselves, break our tendencies by formation, and incorporate well-conceived plays into what we're doing already. Trap plays will be discussed extensively in a future chapter, as

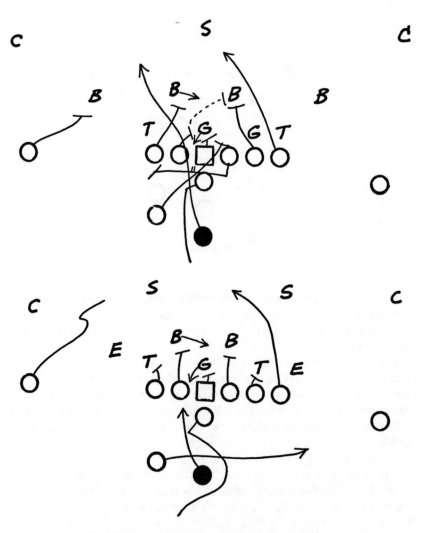

Figure 1-2 "Open T10/Cross fire at 1"
"Open T10/Crossbuck trap at 3"

will our formation-calling system, which is important to an efficient self-scouting format.

Attack defenses are as effective as any defensive strategy when it comes to giving offensive coaches headaches. They do a good job of neutralizing the running game, and they also provide for a very effective pass rush. But they have a tough time with play-action passes and with most any running back who breaks through the front eight. That's why we like either to load up at the point of attack or to allow them to stunt themselves

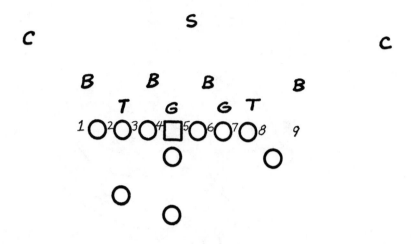

Figure 1-3

away from the ball carrier. Both of these strategies are discussed extensively in future chapters.

Another alternative is to tighten up the formation and wing it in order
to provide more gaps than the defense can cover. Attack defenses don't
like winged or slotted formations. The eight men they have on the
defensive front *still* aren't enough to defend against the nine gaps in
areas that the Wing T presents (see figure 1-3). The problems the Wing
T presents for the attack defense are diagrammed and discussed in the
next chapter, especially as the Wing T provides a balanced run and play-
action passing threat.

CONFUSE THE BLOCKING SCHEMES

A second purpose of attack defenses is to vary positioning in order to
confuse the blocking assignments of the offensive line. The actual alignments really don't matter, as long as the stunts cover the gaps in the line
or provide for contact with all the offensive linemen and serve to confuse
the blocking schemes of the offense. Consider the 4-4 stack alignment
in figure 1-4. Any combination of stunts will be able to defend each gap
along the line, at least eight of the gaps.

The alignment, however, highlights one of the inherent weaknesses
of the 4-4 stack. It doesn't provide much of an outside pass rush, and
it tends to be a step slow when outside containment is required. Because
the outside stack is responsible for *three* gaps versus the Wing T, we like
to attack the outside with a Double cross block. Figure 1-4 illustrates a
"T8/Cross fire QB keep at 8/Double cross."

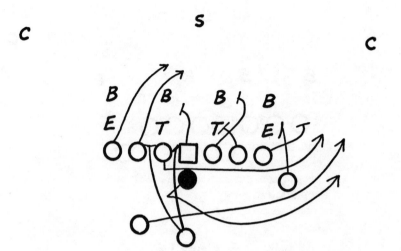

Figure 1-4 "T8/Cross fire QB keep at 8/Double cross"

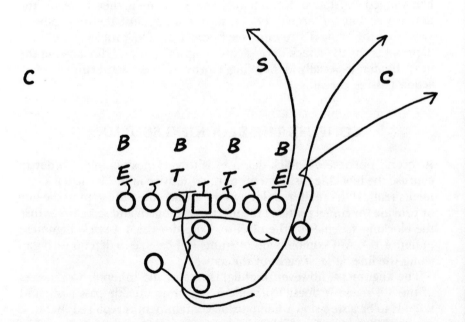

Figure 1-5 "T8/Cross fire QB keep at 8 action/Flood split"

The play gives us two inverted cross blocks on the outside, both of which provide good angles on whichever defender is coming. It sends the fullback up the gut to neutralize the linebackers and to fill for the offside guard, who, along with the left halfback, is providing more blocking to the outside. It's a good play, particularly versus a team that likes the 4-4 stack.

We also complement it with an excellent play-action pass. Figure 1-5 illustrates a "T8/Cross fire QB keep at 8 action/Flood split." The passing play complements the running play in every way and exploits two of the 4-4's weakest elements, a questionable outside pass rush and a susceptibility to the play-action pass. It isn't a bomb either. The wingback is running just deep enough to influence the cornerback. The left halfback can receive the pass as soon as he enters the secondary.

Obviously, the success of the play depends on the stalking skills of the pass receivers, effective fire-out blocking on the line, and convincing backfield faking. As with any good play-action passing attack, pass receivers should become pass *deceivers*. If they execute their "sell jobs" convincingly, particularly versus a three-deep attack defense, the offense has a "better-than-guessing" chance to put points on the board. An entire chapter will be devoted to an effective play-action passing attack later in the book.

GANGING UP

If the opponent has determined that we like to run the off-tackle hole at certain times during a game, we can count on the fact that he is going to try to plug it up, usually by stunting into it. Very infrequently will even the most confident attack defense position itself in an overloaded alignment, unless it shifts out of it before the snap of the ball.

It may give us some kind of a 4-4 set or may even use a split-6, one of today's most popular defenses. Both provide the opportunity to overload the off-tackle hole, while protecting the rest of the line of scrimmage. First, let's look at what the defense might do with the 4-4. Figure 1-6 illustrates an odd-look 4-4 set with an outside scrape. If, in fact, our play is attacking the off-tackle hole, we could be in a lot of trouble.

Oh, we can be real smart *now* and say that we would exit block with the end and have the wingback step through. We do just that often. But attack defenses are generally too smart, so at times we get hammered by a defensive stunt—until we get the time to make whatever adjustments are necessary.

A game just last year serves as an excellent example. Instead of using a 4-4 set, our opponent was in a split-6, but the result was the same. As

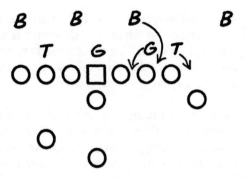

Figure 1-6 "Offset 4-4/Outside scrape/Strongside"

illustrated in figure 1-7, he kept jamming our four hole with the onside linebacker, who was scraping with the down guard.

It was a good stunt. The opponent knew that we liked cross fire action with our fullback, so he consistently jammed the one and two holes with the defensive guards. He did, in fact, stop our fullback. He also stopped cross fire action everywhere else along the line of scrimmage because the linebacker was getting an open door into the backfield.

During the first half, we managed to hold our own because we reverted to a lot of power action to the outside. It provided the down-blocking we needed to pick up the linebacker, and it caught the defensive tackle's outside slant with a double team block. We didn't need to "plateau" with

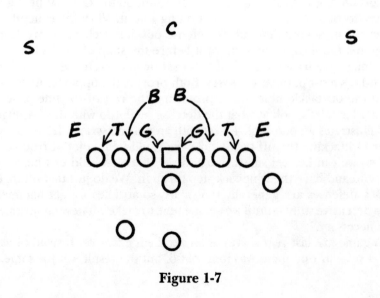

Figure 1-7

the offensive end because the linebacker was stunting himself into the line anyway. That, combined with some quick action and the three or four plays our fullback managed to break up the gut, gave us a tie score at halftime.

We already knew what the defense was doing, but we asked the offensive line to tell us anyway. We like to have the kids hustle while they wait. Our philosophy has always been, "We'll either find a way—or make one." If the kids are involved in the decision, they have more invested in the solution when they take the field.

If you're *really* lucky, one of the players will suggest the solution you already have in mind. Fortunately, that's what happened on the day in question. Interestingly enough, it was our fullback who asked, "Why don't we go into the Pro 4?"

Figure 1-8 illustrates a "Pro 4/Quick at 4." Don't worry about the formation designations or the names of our series at this point. More will be said about them later, when we describe our system of self-scouting. For now, just recognize that we decided to fight fire with fire. So we aligned four players against their *three* defenders at the four hole. Fundamentally, if you want to break through the enemy lines, what do you do? You overload at one point and pound away. We decided to hit them right where they *thought* they were the strongest.

With this page out of Eisenhower's book, we told our right guard to take the man who stunts to the inside. It was an easy block because the down tackle came to the gap most often. The guard simply allowed him to fight to the inside gap, in effect, *away* from the point of attack. The tackle took the man on his head; he also was fighting to slant away from

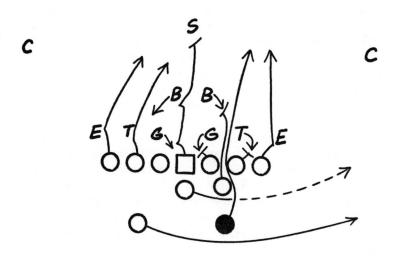

Figure 1-8 "Pro 4/Quick at 4"

the point of attack. Finally, we instructed the center to inside release, looking for the offside linebacker. If he was coming, block him. If he was stunting away, go right for the safety.

The fullback made the play go. We positioned him between the offensive guard and tackle, about a yard off the line of scrimmage, and told him to pick up whoever came to the inside, usually the onside linebacker. All the fullback had to do was take one position step with his right foot while reading the linebacker's initial move.

The "Pro 4/Quick at 4" and the "Pro 3/Quick at 3" picked up *literally* seven to ten yards per play. It gave us a quick score early in the second half and, most important, drove them out of their favorite defense. They tried one or two other stunts, but the Pro 4 provides for such a wide variety of play calls, we weren't bothered for the remainder of the game. It's distinctive feature is that it provides for an overload in the middle of the line of scrimmage, just where it's needed to compensate for most of the stunts that an attack defense can throw at you.

A FOCUS

The Pro 4 formation is going to be a focal point of this book. No single concept, aside from a few very successful blocking strategies, has provided us as much *consistent* success against attack defenses. Think about it. Attack defenses, as mentioned already, are capable of defending against eight areas along the line of scrimmage. The Wing T formation gives them *nine*. The Pro 4 puts the ninth right in the middle of the line, where most attack defenses believe themselves to be their strongest.

It can provoke the defense into some serious adjustments, particularly when they're not prepared for it. We have never maintained a steady diet of the Pro 4, but we have used it extensively for several years now and have developed a variety of sophisticated plays to use with it. Many of them will be diagrammed and discussed in future chapters. We have even developed plays from the Pro 2 or the T 2 formations. They provide the same dimension.

The plays are well conceived. They give us most of our offensive, some interesting pass plays, and some of the quickest-hitting counter plays in football. You will find them easy to incorporate into your offense, and, who knows, you might even want to use one or two of *our* plays. Certainly, *any* unanticipated formation causes attack defenses some initial concerns, but the Pro 4 and Pro 2 sets introduce not only unique formations for them to key, but strong interior alignments that can create blocking mismatches.

THE 4-4

The team that is not afraid to gamble—or *has* to—will often use some variation of the 4-4. They may stack, straight up or in the gaps, or they may stagger the positioning. Regardless of the alignment, you can bet they will be coming from every possible direction. The line may slant one way, the linebackers another; tandems may stunt independently of the others; or the line may slant and the linebackers read. Whatever they do, they can cause problems with the line blocking.

For that reason, when we use any of our regular formations with the fullback in his home position, we make a lot of use of the "blast" call, particularly from the T 2 formation. Figure 1-9 illustrates an "Open T 2/Fullback Blast." The backfield action is Cross fire, but the fullback doesn't go to either the one or the two hole. He runs straight behind the center, who snaps the ball and races between the two stacks, looking for an off-colored jersey. The key to the play is the block of the back in the two position.

Obviously, the line is instructed to get wider than normal splits, up to four feet. The two back is instructed to follow the center and to block any off-colored jersey to show. Both guards are told to inside-release on the stacks and to block either of the players to come to the inside. If the defensive guards are trying to jam the gaps, the offensive guards are instructed to block them. If one or both of the defensive linemen are

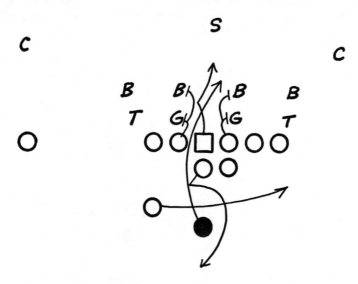

Figure 1-9 "Open T2/Fullback blast"

slanting out toward the tackle, the guards are instructed to keep going and to pick up the linebacker(s). We have found that a defensive guard looping to his outside will never recover fast enough to trip up a fullback who is racing directly behind the center.

In essence, when we blast block, we look to block just one of the two men in the stack. We disregard the other. If the defense is instructed to compensate for our big line splits by going into the gap, we're in a natural position to two-team the onside defensive guard with our right guard and center and to kick out the linebacker with the two back. That's the strength of the formation. See figure 1-10 for an illustration.

The fullback doesn't do much differently from his regular crossfire responsibility. He cheats up a step or two and runs straight ahead, reading either the center's or the two back's block. Both he and the quarterback must be aware of the possibility of the inside stack going into a gap because of the wide line splits. The fullback will have to run the ball somewhat wider than normal. That, however, is the only adjustment.

If both defensive guards pinch, we can be in a little trouble. Even with good line splits, it can get pretty crowded in the middle. But if only one pinches or both loop to the outside, we're likely to pick up pretty good yardage. If the stack goes into the gap, we're in very good shape.

We can never predict what an attack defense is going to do at any given time, but if we do a good job scouting ourselves—a process that will be discussed in a later chapter—we can come close to being right often enough to cause the defense a lot of trouble. The least we can do is to chase them out of one of their favorite alignments. Regardless of

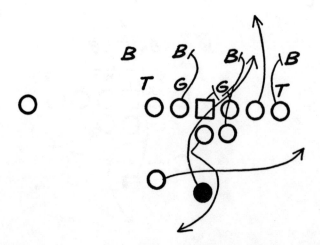

Figure 1-10 "Fullback blast versus adjusted gap stack"

their adjustment to the wide-line splits, the back in the two position gives us whatever blocking we need to open up the inside.

Blast blocking with the two and four alignments can also be used for quarterback sneaks and for any quick opener action at three or four. The principles are fundamentally the same. All the plays using blast blocking are described in a later chapter. Remember, we don't use it as a steady diet. You won't either, but it's a very effective change of pace that is not only fun to use but "discomforting" to most attack defenses.

THE NINTH AREA

As mentioned earlier, attack defenses realize that their homework is cut out for them whenever they play a team using a Wing T. They have a tough time covering that ninth area on the line of scrimmage. So we like to exploit it once in a while, particularly at the perimeter. Any fair-thinking defensive coach, even the most devout advocate of attack defenses, will acknowledge that the 4-4 stack is a relatively weak containment defense.

Figure 1-11 illustrates a "Pro 8/Power right/Double outside." Normal power action would involve a double team on the defensive tackle and the fullback blocking the outside man on the line of scrimmage. The "Double outside" involves the tackle in an area block and the end and wingback in a double-team block on the man to show on the outside. The fullback and offside guard then lead the play around the end.

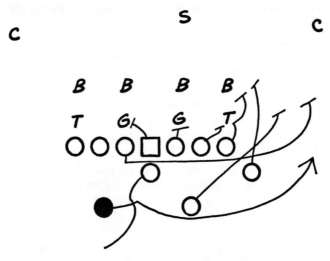

Figure 1-11 "Pro 8/Power right/Double outside"

The blocking scheme provides an excellent strategy for turning the corner but invariably has chased the defense out of their outside stack. Normally, they adjust the outside backer to a head-up position on our wingback, or, more often, go into a completely different defensive alignment.

That's the beauty of beating an attack defense. They're gambling anyway. They may try to cover their tails in predetermined ways, but no defense is foolproof. Each has strengths and weaknesses. If we find the weaknesses often enough, we can chase the defense out of one of its favorite alignments. That's a big step toward a winning effort.

CONFUSING THE MONSTER

So far, we've emphasized the fact that attack defenses come in all shapes and sizes and operate on the premise that their best bet is to "make something happen." The basic alignment is one thing; what they plan to do from it is another. But there's one thing we can be sure of. They're going to come at us—from every direction. And they're going to make use of scouting reports to pattern their stunts. They're also going to make basic assumptions.

One assumption seems to be that offensive teams run into the strength of their formations most of the time. That seems to be a reasonable assumption, particularly because it's proven empirically every time we watch a football game. So again it seems logical that attack defenses that use monster men will position them to the strong side of the offensive formation.

Consider the team that uses a 5-2 with a monster, and, in effect, becomes an overshifted 6-2. Figure 1-12 illustrates an overshifted 6-2 versus a T 8 formation. The defense retains the advantage of having a stunting noseman, with the additional variation of both inside and outside scrape maneuvers with the linebackers. Finally, positioning the monster man to the strongside of the formation isn't a bad idea because we all know that most of the game's action will come that way.

But what happens to such a defense when the offensive formation shows no strongside? The defensive game plan doesn't do much good, and one of their toughest football players will start feeling like the Lone Ranger when the action keeps going the other way. If the Wing T formation causes problems for an attack defense, imagine what the double wing does. It provides *ten* areas to be covered—by eight men.

In addition, consider the fact that most attack defenses employing a monster man slant the line away from the monster to compensate for their short-handedness on the weakside of the formation. That added

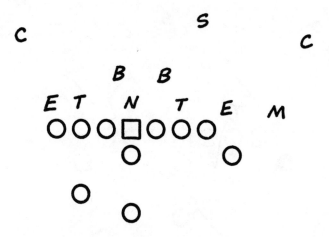

Figure 1-12 "Overshifted 6"

bit of knowledge can give a double wing offense unfair advantage, particularly if the defense is unprepared for the formation.

Figure 1-13 illustrates a "Double Wing/Motion left/Power left" against an overshifted 6-2. Assume that the monster is lining up to the *long* side of the field, given the fact that he has few other clues as to where the ball is likely to be run. All we do is put the right wing in one-second motion back to his original position and run anything we want, in this case a power left—*away* from the monster.

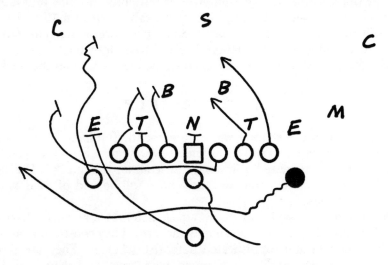

Figure 1-13 "Double wing/Motion left/Power left"

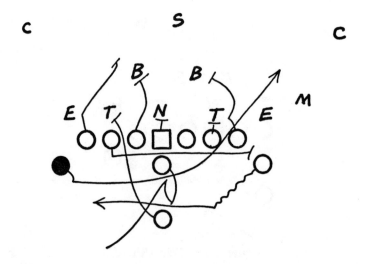

Figure 1-14 "Double wing/Motion left/Power Counter at 6"

If we want to get *really* nasty later on, when the monster and the secondary begin to adjust, we'll use the same formation, with the same motion, only, after we've conditioned the defense, we'll call a "Power counter at six," as diagrammed in figure 1-14. It provides for down blocks and a tackle trap, both of which are very effective against attack defenses.

The double wing with motion gives us our entire offense, and it tells the defense nothing regarding our tendencies by formation. Just imagine what it does for the passing game. Some plays are better than others from the double wing formation. We'll discuss all of them—as well as their strategic effectiveness versus attack defenses—later in the book.

LET'S WRAP IT UP

Our purpose in this chapter was to describe the fundamental purposes of most attack defenses and to outline a few ways that teams try to realize them. We also suggested a few ways to "counter the attack." The suggestions were only illustrative. Much more will be said of each as the book progresses.

So, when all is said and done, attack defenses take their share of gambles, and they come in all shapes and sizes. They consist of a myriad of fancy names and sophisticated defensive schemes. They use terms like scrape, crash, go, fire, jam, pinch, blitz, cross, and slant, and they attack from every angle. They'll attack from a variety of defensive alignments: 4-4, 5-2, 5-3, 6-2. The face may be different, but the game's the same: attack, penetrate, and confuse; everything we've discussed in this chapter.

Our purpose is to counter the attack, to swing the odds in our favor. An understanding of our opponent is critical. An understanding of *ourselves* is as important. No high-stakes poker player ever got past the ante without carefully evaluating his opponents or without a controlled understanding of his own strengths and weaknesses. Certainly, he wasn't in much of a position to call any bluffs.

That's precisely what the offense wants to do with attack defenses. Let *them* do all the gambling. We'll search out their weaknesses and exploit them every chance we get. Clearly, we'll never predict with one-hundred percent confidence just what the defense is going to do at any given moment. But we can exploit a few weaknesses in each alignment. A knowledgeable use of the Wing T will help, so let's take a look at it.

2

Countering the Attack: Exploiting the Wing T

Admittedly, attack defenses pose serious problems for offensive coaches. The problems can become insurmountable if we don't keep in mind several important principles to guide our behavior. One of the most useful of these was stated quite clearly years ago by a gentleman who probably cared little about football, but who generally found a way to penetrate to the core of a problem. Robert Frost said: "The best way out is always *through*." We might add that *over* isn't a bad idea either. The Wing T provides the opportunity to do both: go through and over.

The Wing T, irrespective of the backfield set, provides a strong running formation to one side and a strong passing formation to the other. Simple realignment in the backfield might make one or the other a stronger offensive threat, but the compound problem for the defense remains. Whether the backfield alignment is balanced, as with the "I" and "Pro" sets in figure 2-1, or is slightly *im*balanced as in figure 2-2, the running and the passing threat remain constant.

The combined threats of the formation involve even more trouble for the defense if the offense is willing to capitalize on the basic unpredictability of the wing formation. Coaches who adopt the Wing T and then play "grind-it-out" football just aren't using their heads. Either that, or they're blessed with young giants whose hearts fill up their chest cavities.

Given the improbability of *that* kind of good fortune, let's just assume that the offensive coach who falls into a predictable pattern of play-calling compromises the inherent strength of the Wing T. He establishes obvious tendencies that even the most muddled attack defense can stop.

Then, if he makes the additional mistake of emphasizing the run on the first two downs and the pass on the third, he becomes even more

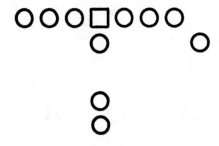

Figure 2-1 "Pro 8"
"I8"

predictable. "Unpredictability," therefore, is the word. The astute offensive coach will coordinate a well-sequenced running game and a complementary play-action passing attack. He will further complement his attack with an array of misdirection plays that create the illusion of his basic series. Then he will study his opponents' defensive tendencies and attack them with the proper play at the weakest spot in the defense.

Sound simple? Well, maybe it's not *that* easy. If it were, none of us would be able to find the challenge in football that keeps us sticking our noses into books like this one. But it's not all that difficult either, particularly if we keep one simple fact in mind—and seek to capitalize on it whenever we can.

THE NINTH GAP

All eight-man defensive fronts—the usual staple of most attack defenses—are able to cover only eight gaps along the line of scrimmage by definition! It may come as no startling revelation to you, but it is a recurring and somewhat disturbing reality to the defensive coach who has to cover the *nine* gaps in the Wing T.

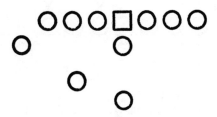

Figure 2-2 "Wing 7"

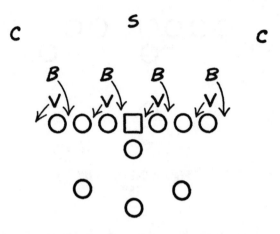

Figure 2-3 "4-4 Stack"

Figure 2-3 illustrates a standard balanced formation with a full-house backfield. If the defense employs a stack 4-4 with a line slant and a linebacker fill-type stunt, it can plug each gap along the line of scrimmage. It can even provide fair containment to the outside, although that is one of its weaknesses. It's also trappable, but we will discuss that later.

If the offense lines up in a Wing T, it provides a *ninth* gap that an eight-man front is unable to cover. Figure 2-4 illustrates our T 8 formation and the same 4-4 stack. For the sake of discussion, if it were to slant its line charge and adjust with its linebackers as in figure 2-3, it would be unable to contain to the outside on the winged side of the offensive formation.

Obviously, all 4-4 stacks don't stunt so predictably, nor do they always remain in the stacked formation versus a winged offensive set. Normally,

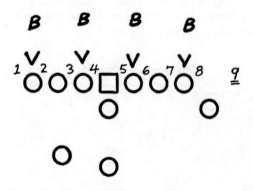

Figure 2-4 "T8"

they have to make some kind of an adjustment, which is advantage number one of the Wing T. It communicates to opposing coaches that their work is cut out for them, and, even before the toss of the coin, it causes them to question the advisability of their defensive set.

PRINCIPLE NUMBER ONE: EXPLOIT THE NINTH GAP

Figure 2-5 illustrates an "Inside belly at 6, Bend block." It's one of the several plays that enables us to exploit the relatively weak containment potential of the eight-man defensive front, particularly when the defensive end/outside backer keys the movements of the offensive end. By using our Wing T formation, in this case a T 8, we overload the outside right and exploit the defensive techniques that represent the opponent's bread and butter. The very techniques he assumes are his strengths become his weaknesses.

If we outside-release the right end, we find that we don't have to block the outside man. This, of course, is true only if the outside man on the defensive line is keying the movements of the offensive end. If he's keying the backfield, we have other blocking schemes we can employ, each of which can be called by our offensive tackle. They will be discussed later. For now, let's assume the outside man is keying the end.

In addition, let's also assume that the defense doesn't have to align itself in a predictable defensive set. Depending on down and distance or field position, they may opt for a variable alignment, let's say a 4-4. The bend block is still appropriate because it outside-releases the end

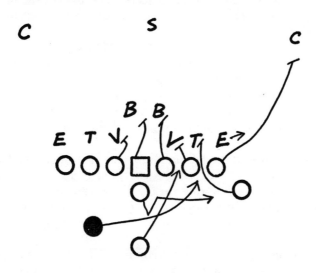

Figure 2-5

and instructs him to block whichever man in the tandem goes to the outside.

The wingback blocks whichever of the two goes to the inside. In effect, the blocking scheme provides angles for the wingback and the offensive tackle. The tackle is instructed to block whichever player in the tandem goes to the outside. The guard takes the player stunting to the inside.

The proper position steps for each player are critical if both are to area-block the tandem effectively. Because the guard is to protect the inside seam, he is told to step hard with his left foot, anticipating contact from the defensive tackle. If the tackle comes, he is instructed to pivot hard off his position step in order to square up with the defensive charge. Then he simply prevents penetration. We don't need a form block from him, just enough shield to keep the defensive tackle out of the backfield.

If the defensive tackle doesn't come, the guard is instructed to follow with his right foot and to look for the linebacker on an inside blitz. If the linebacker is not on a predetermined stunt and is reading the backfield action, the guard is instructed to try to get a piece of him. So is the fullback. *While he is completing his fake,* he is to run into the player in the tandem who does *not* stunt to the inside. The fullback gives us an additional blocker on either the linebacker or the defensive tackle, and, most important, it gives us an excellent fake.

The onside tackle is instructed to take a position step with his left foot directly at the defensive tackle. If the tackle comes, the offensive man puts his helmet on the man's numbers and drives him away from the point of attack. If the defensive tackle slants toward the guard, the tackle drives off his position step and adjusts his path toward the onside linebacker, who will be moving by precommitment or by adjustment to the backfield flow.

The skills involve relatively simple area-blocking techniques. It's a constant source of amazement to us, however, that so many otherwise excellent linemen cannot execute these techniques with consistency. The problem was a concern to us years ago when inside linebackers in the 5-2 started scraping with the noseman or the tackle. But we learned to accommodate that with modified pass-blocking strategies to prevent inside penetration.

The advent of the attack defense, however, has transformed a concern into a critical issue. The defense is charging from so many different directions and with such a wide variety of stunting techniques that fundamentals have become our primary concern. Coach Barry Switzer, the growing legend at Oklahoma, once told us that great players make great plays.

Who can deny the validity of his comment? Give us the aggregate of backfield talent that he has year after year, and we, too, might come up with a win-loss record that makes most coaches shake their heads in disbelief. So, we may not have the abundance of blue-chippers that populate "Switzer-land," but we *can* refine the fundamental skills of the equally dedicated, if less talented kids we work with.

LEARNING IS DOING

We discovered the answer in learning research, specifically in modality learning. "The day of the dumb football player is over." So is the day of the benighted football coach. The days of depriving kids of water during mid-summer practice sessions to "make them tough" are long gone. They disappeared about the same time we decided to let football players wear face masks—even if they didn't have broken noses. We finally learned that football players can be tough and *safe* at the same time.

We also learned that there's a whole lot more to this game than three yards and a cloud of astroturf. Kids learn in different ways. Some learn better with their eyes, others with their ears, and still others with their bodies. The key phrase nowadays has become "Tell me, I forget; show me, I remember; *involve* me—I learn."

To emphasize the importance and the significant learning potential within the kinesthetic modality, we devote a lot of time to simple drills that walk each athlete through the proper technique. The proper fundamentals in mastering area-blocking techniques, therefore, begin with the proper offensive stance followed by a deliberate position step and the appropriate follow-up steps, emphasizing body positioning and solid base.

At first, the steps are taken at one-quarter speed, then half-speed, then full speed. The duration of the process is contingent on the levels of observable mastery. We may spend a week or two during the early part of the season gradually progressing from "walking through it" to one-on-one contact drills.

Like so many English teachers who assume that *lecturing* about the religious symbolism in *Moby Dick* is the same as *teaching* the book, we had assumed early in our careers that telling a kid, even *showing* him, was all that was involved in *coaching* him. Fortunately, we discovered that some of our kids fell woefully short in the study of world literature because their auditory and visual modalities were weak. Maybe that's one of the reasons they opted for the physical outlet of football. Some of them are kinesthetic *geniuses*.

So we don't *tell* them, nor do we simply *show* them. We *involve* them, and we capitalize on the kinesthetic brainpower they bring to each practice session. Step by step; walking through it, then running through it— that's the key.

We'll do the same thing with our ends to teach proper pass patterns. Consider the last play, the inside belly at 6. It provides great backfield action for a complementary play-action pass, one that is real trouble for attack defenses, particularly because it does such a great job complementing the bend block.

PRINCIPLE NUMBER TWO: EXPLOIT THE HOLES IN THE SECONDARY

If we capitalize on principle number one long and hard enough, the defense will start attacking the seams with greater abandon. They recognize that they are outmanned anyway, so they are likely to send the linebackers on a steady diet of scrapes and blitzes. They may even send the safety occasionally.

How you get them to adopt such a kamikaze mentality is up to you and the sophistication of your offensive attack. We will provide more help later in the book with alternative offensive alignments and specific plays designed to create the ninth gap at different places on the line of scrimmage. For now, however, let's assume that the running game has been pounding on them with at least moderate success. They may have held you to no gain or a play or two, but they had to rely on their stunting linebackers to do that.

Here's where principle number two comes into play. Blitzing linebackers leave voids in the hook zones. They help provide a pretty strong pass rush, but they leave the flat and the hook zones wide open. If we can execute our play-action passes so that they appear initially identical to the running play they are designed to complement, we are going to place the defense in a no-win situation.

That's why we use the same step-by-step process with play-action passes that we use with area-blocking techniques. Figure 2-6 illustrates an "Inside belly at 6 action-right Alabama." The backfield action is identical to the running play; so are the initial moves of the offensive right end and the wingback.

The important thing to keep in mind with this play is the complementarity between running action and passing action. That play-action passes require very careful and deliberate execution comes as no startling revelation to the veteran football coach. If *any* component of the play—the pass routes, the line blocking, or the backfield faking—falls short of near-perfect execution, the play will deceive no one, and the element of unpredictability will be lost to the offense.

So we walk the players through each of their maneuvers *before* we expect them to use the play in scrimmage or even to execute it full speed in an introductory drill. The offensive right end and the wingback must

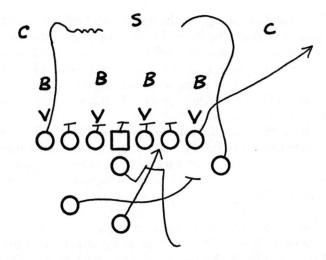

Figure 2-6 "T8/Inside belly at 6/Right Alabama"

sell their "bend" blocking techniques. The right end must outside-release toward the onside cornerback, thereby influencing both the outside man on the defensive line and the cornerback. He probably will influence the safety, too, particularly if the safety is keying him for pass action.

The wingback must take his initial position step toward the defensive end and approach him as if to execute his "down blocking" maneuver. If the bend block has been at least moderately successful previously in the game, the defensive lineman will be influenced by the wingback's initial movement. This will accomplish two things.

PASS DECEIVERS

One, it will sell "run" to anyone in the secondary who is keying the wingback's movement. This probably is the most important element within the play. It reaffirms the reality that pass receivers when executing *play-action* routes must first be pass *deceivers*. They must convince everyone in the secondary that they are positioning themselves for a block and that the play is an onside belly at 6. Like the guard and tackle who must use their kinesthetic brainpower to master area-blocking techniques by walking through each phase of its execution, the offensive end and wingback must do the same when learning the initial characteristics of a well-executed play-action pass. We will discuss those characteristics at more length in a future chapter.

The second advantage of the wingback's "sell job" is that it slows up the pass rush from the defensive end. Even the most thoroughly conditioned defensive lineman is influenced by a wingback who embarrasses him early in the game. If the bend block is successful two or three times, the defensive tackle is going to be looking for him once the offensive tackle down blocks. He can't help but be influenced. Human nature still prevails over football strategy.

If the lineman execute convincing fire-out blocks and if the backs sell the inside belly at 6, the play is a winner, especially if it has convinced the defense to send the linebackers in an attempt to penetrate into the backfield. That's why we instruct the wingback to read the linebacker's movements during the early part of the play.

He should look at the onside linebacker as soon as he takes his first position step toward the defensive end. He can watch the defensive end peripherally while he focuses most of his attention on the onside linebacker. If the linebacker stunts, the wingback is instructed to veer off his position step and move diagonally away from the line of scrimmage and into the hook zone vacated by the linebacker.

If the backer *doesn't* stunt, the wingback is instructed to run a short banana in *and out*, moving on a diagonal but *almost* parallel path away from the line of scrimmage and toward the sidelines. The pass path, even when executed away from a linebacker dropping to his hook zone, is very difficult to stop. The safety generally ends up chasing the wingback, *if* he doesn't get sucked up by the fullback's inside belly fake.

The defensive player who *really* finds himself in a bind is the inside cornerback. If the offensive end, wingback, and backfield personnel do a good job selling the inside belly and its blocking action, the linebackers (if they are reading) and the secondary either will be sucked up toward the play action or will be immobilized long enough for the "deceivers" to find the open spaces in the secondary.

The cornerback is in double trouble. He first has to determine if the play is a run or a pass; then he has to chase the offensive right end, who has stalked him momentarily and then has broken past him on a deep pass route along the sidelines. If it is executed well—and any play-action pass involves a big *if*—the play is very hard to stop. More about the execution of effective play-action passes will be discussed in a future chapter.

For now, let us just acknowledge the complementarity of two plays that do a pretty good job complicating the problems of even the best attack defense. The point to be emphasized is that a complementary relationship must exist between and around all the plays used versus attack defenses. They may *seem* to be attacking randomly, but their movements are all coordinated, and, most important, *someone* is reading *some* element of the backfield action.

Timing and well-coordinated execution are equally critical for the offense. If any component of the offense takes "the play off" or confuses its assignment, neither play will do what it is designed to do. The defense's job will be that much easier. Once we start making the defense's job easy, we're in real trouble. So let's work long and hard on precise execution. It's particularly important for the misdirection element in this particular sequence.

PRINCIPLE THREE: USE MISDIRECTION TO ATTACK THE WEAK SIDE

The inside belly counter is a great complement to the basic play, particularly if the defense becomes overly conscious of the strong side of the offensive formation. Teams that employ a monster man are particularly vulnerable to misdirection, in this instance the "inside belly counter at 5," runs from the same formation, the T 8.

Figure 2-7 illustrates the play and reveals the dilemma the defense faces. The defense is a 6 with a monster and generally does a good job not only confusing offensive assignments but stopping a wide variety of basic plays. "Countering the attack," however, doesn't involve a basic play. It involves a well-conceived attack on the weak-side defensive end with one of our quickest hitting misdirection plays.

Again, the formation is a T 8, and the call is an "Inside belly counter at 5." The play can be exceptionally effective for two important reasons. One, it uses a pulling tackle, not a guard. Versus most defenses that key

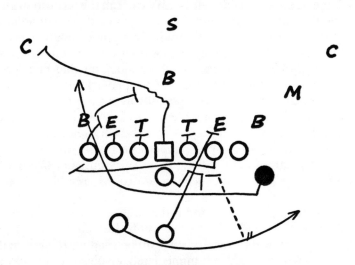

Figure 2-7 "T8/Inside belly counter at 5"

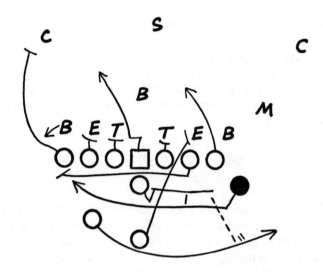

Figure 2-8 "T8/Inside belly counter at 5/Outside release"

the triangle as well as backfield action, a pulling tackle doesn't provide the linebackers an immediate indication of the direction of the play. It also provides the tackles an opportunity to get out of the trenches, forget the hand-to-hand combat, and launch an armored attack on an unsuspecting defensive end.

The only modification in the blocking scheme would involve the offensive left end. Figure 2-8 illustrates the same play, only with the offensive left end on an outside release. We can call the tactic in the huddle or provide the option to the end if he gets jammed every time he down blocks on the defensive man to his inside. If the defensive man is reading the end's reaction, the outside-release will set up the defensive man for the tackle's trap block, and the two-team block on that man probably will be unnecessary due to the angle of his penetration.

The only real problem for the play involves the possibility of penetration up the middle. If the middle linebacker "deals" with one of the linemen and somehow finds his way into the backfield, he can stop the play cold by tripping up the pulling tackle or by catching the wingback before he gets started. The center, therefore, must not fire out at the middle linebacker but must execute a controlled area block to prevent penetration.

If he executes a good block and if the fullback does his sell job at the off-tackle hole, the middle linebacker will be influenced away from the point of attack. So will the safety who will be reading the left halfback. Because the left halfback is not immediately involved in the play action and actually is moving away from the point of attack, the play is strategically appropriate for a defense that is overly conscious of the offensive alignment's strong side.

We have had considerable success with it. Like all misdirection plays, it allows us to run away from the strongside of our formation and to increase the element of unpredictability in our offense. Once our unpredictability has been established, we have reaffirmed the strength of our basic offense and have provoked more than a little doubt in the opponent's belief in his defense.

PRINCIPLE FOUR: CAPITALIZE
ON UNPREDICTABILITY

The need for unpredictability also has led us to complement our inside belly counter with pass action. Figure 2-9 illustrates a "T 8/Inside belly counter at 5 action pass." It is designed to beat the onside cornerback and safety who react quickly to a wingback moving back on counter action to the weak side of the offensive formation. Most attack defenses will precommit the line to patterned movements, but the secondary has to continue keying certain offensive players. And we key *them*.

Offensive coaches are well advised to capitalize on those keys. The counter-action pass, irrespective of backfield action, does it as well as any play in our playbook. If the ends do a good job stalking the defense

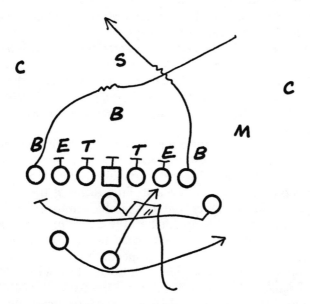

Figure 2-9 "T8/Inside belly counter at 5 action pass"

before they release into their pass routes, the secondary can be in a real bind, particularly if the safety is a "hit man" who likes to stick his nose into run action and if he's been burned once or twice with the counter play.

We can burn him if the backfield does a good job selling the inside belly, if the line executes good fire-out blocks, and if the ends appear initially to be blocking their respective men on defense. Obviously, the success of the play is dependent on several different variables. That's the primary reason why we devote so much practice time to the proper execution of play-action passes.

We will practice our conventional drop-back passing attack on one day and our play-action attack on another. The pass paths are substantially different in each attack, so to emphasize that difference, we're careful to practice them differently. On conventional passing days, all those line coaches who are convinced they can coach quarterbacks get their chance. After they've checked to be certain the line is effectively area-blocking defensive stunts, particularly in dummy scrimmage, all the coaches can watch the passers and receivers and can hand out all those enlightening pointers that they have been saving up all summer.

But they have to watch the line on every play when we practice our play-action passing attack. The line must develop the habit of firing out into the defensive man, whether he's holding an air-flate or whether he's scratching to get to the quarterback. Linemen must not develop the habit of pass blocking during play-action passing. A pass block is a sure giveaway to the sharp player in the secondary whose peripheral vision enables him to pick up more than just his key.

Similarly, the backfield coach has to watch the backfield faking as well as the quarterback's execution. Any back who hustles through a fake to get to his block compromises the entire play, and not just by making a lousy fake. By racing through his responsibility, he probably will force the quarterback to move faster, thereby forcing the quarterback to show pass sooner.

The problem doesn't end there. If the exact timing of the play isn't assured during each and every practice, the receivers are likely to race through their patterns and forget to stalk the defenders. At that point, the play is obviously a pass, even to little Suzie in the stands, who is interested only in how cute Tom looks in his uniform.

To compound the problem further, the entire process is just as true in reverse. If the receivers come out of the blocks like world-class sprinters and run their pass routes at top speed, the quarterback is going to race through his fakes to be able to throw the ball before the receivers get out of range. This, in turn, will force the backs to make bad fakes.

It is important to recognize, therefore, the interdependence of all the players. One athlete—out of sync with the rest—causes a chain reaction that compromises the entire play. That's why we practice play-action passes and conventional passes on different days. More will be said about play-action passes in a later chapter.

For now, just recognize that the line blocking, the backfield faking, and the stalking techniques of the receivers are all critical if the play in figure 2-9 is going to help "counter the attack." The offensive left end, for example, who probably is the play's primary receiver, must hesitate for two counts before he releases into his pass route. If he delays long enough and actually gets hidden in the line, he is certain to be open underneath the secondary coverage, especially if the linebackers are coming.

Without that necessary delay, the essence of Principle Four, "Capitalize on Unpredictability," is lost in a burst of obvious intentions. Once the offense becomes obvious, it's in a lot of trouble.

LET'S WRAP IT UP

We haven't even discussed the wide variety of trap plays the Wing T formation gives us. We will focus on them in a later chapter. Nor did we discuss several alignment variations that are available to us. They, too, will be discussed later. We *did* discuss four principles we use to guide our play-calling versus attack defenses. The first involved the general idea of exploiting the ninth gap created on the line of scrimmage by the Wing T formation. Obviously, a multitude of strategies are available to us. We discussed just a couple. We will discuss the others later.

The important thing to keep in mind, however, is the principle itself. Your offense may be different from ours. That's not to say that you are unable to incorporate our plays into your offense. Take all you want; they're adaptable to almost any offense. It's just that you will discover elements within your own offense that will exploit the ninth gap. The principle is the thing. Keep it in mind; it can lead to all kinds of exciting and effective strategies.

The same is true of the other principles we mentioned in this chapter. The idea of finding the holes in the secondary is always a good one, particularly versus a three-deep and a "go-get-'em" type front eight. The elements of misdirection and unpredictability are closely related and will involve considerable overlap in future chapters, but unpredictability involves a whole lot more than misdirection, so we identified the various elements as separate principles.

Future chapters will discuss more principles and will expand on these four at greater length. All the principles have been "field tested" and have survived with high levels of reliability. Obviously, they relate most to questions of strategy, but their *real* success is grounded in their execution. The best-conceived play in football won't gain a yard if the players don't know how to execute it. So the proper fundamentals will remain an important part of our focus, just as they are in each of your practice sessions.

However, strategy is why you joined us, so let's take a quick look at the *double* wing and the problems it poses for attack defenses.

3

The Double Wing: Double Trouble for the Defense

The Wing T, if used strategically, can give attack defenses a lot more than they care to think about. For that reason, we will use it as our primary formation throughout the remainder of the book. It creates that critical ninth gap on the line of scrimmage and gives us a variety of backfield sets from which to run our offense. We stick with it throughout much of the season, and against more traditional defenses. The complementary run and pass threats that it provides give us a strong foundation to start from.

PRINCIPLE NUMBER FIVE: PROVIDE A TENTH GAP

We use other formations as well, particularly for critical games. The *double* wing is one of them. We believe firmly that if the Wing T can bring an attack defense to the edge of lunacy, a double wing can push them over. It provides *ten* gaps along the line of scrimmage that the average 8-man defensive front has to cover, and, as important, it reveals no tendencies by formation.

What could be more disconcerting to the average defensive coach than to analyze game films for hours only to learn that the double wing you've decided to use against him doesn't reveal any tendencies? His problem is complicated further if he uses a monster man, and suddenly doesn't know where to position him. We use other formations as well and will discuss them in further chapters. The double wing has been so much fun for us, however, that we will focus on it in this chapter.

En route to the state championship game a few years ago, we ran into one of the toughest opponents we've ever faced. A perennial power in

Illinois, they were big, fast, and well coached. If that combination isn't devastating enough, they rounded things out by bringing to the game one of the state's most impressive winning traditions. We're pretty proud of our tradition, too, but we were allegedly outmanned on the line, so we entered the game a slight underdog.

We had used the Wing T all year, and we knew full well that our opposing coach would do his homework. We were certain that he would pinpoint our offensive tendencies and pattern his 5-2 monster defense to stop them. Our strategy was simple—yet complete.

We ran our entire offense from the double wing with motion. Actually, it wasn't our *entire* offense, because the single back prevented us from running our quick-opener series, but we used everything else with considerable success. Figure 3-1 illustrates one of our most successful plays, the "Motion left/Cross fire QB keep at 7."

As evidenced in the diagram, the play involves a simple overload on the left side of the formation, with the motion man leading the way for the quarterback, and the left wing down-blocking the first defensive man in the tandem to show to the outside. The left tackle and left guard area block their tandem, and the center simply picks up any penetration from the offside tandem.

It's a simple play but generally pretty effective, particularly against attack defenses that may set the monster to the wide side of the field versus the double wing—as in Figure 3-2. The blocking scheme to the outside provides angles for everyone and, as in Figure 3-1, establishes an excellent foundation of the play-action passing complement.

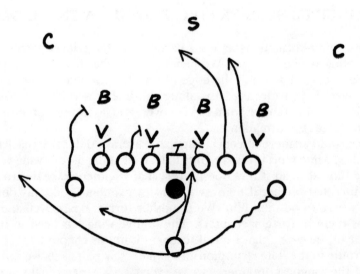

Figure 3-1 "Motion left/XF QB keep at 7"

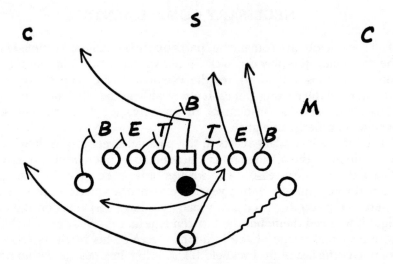

Figure 3-2 "Motion left/XF QB keep at 7"

Figure 3-3 illustrates the "Motion left/Cross fire QB keep at 7/left Delaware." The play is executed exactly like its running complement, even to the point of the pass "deceivers" stalking the same men in the secondary. The rest of the work is up to the line and the right halfback and quarterback. They all must convince the players in the secondary that the quarterback is running the ball around the left end.

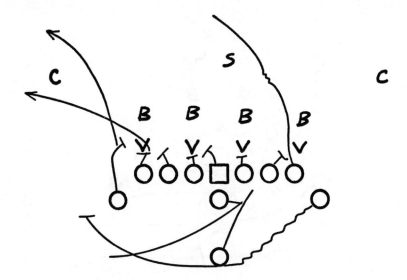

Figure 3-3 "Motion left/XF QB keep at 7/Left Delaware"

NECESSARY COMPLEMENTS

If all the sell jobs are convincing, particularly the stalking maneuvers on the secondary, the play can pick up big yardage. But more important, for our purposes, it illustrates the essential relationship between the running and the passing games. It also reaffirms the importance of using play-action passes against attack defenses, especially when they send everyone in the front eight.

Even if the secondary reacts to the pass deceivers just as their coach wants them to, the offside end is a sure bet to be open in the hook zone. That's the primary reason why we use only seven or eight basic pass plays throughout the entire year. We want the quarterback to know where every receiver is on every play. We have variations on the basic eight if we need them, but the fact remains that the quarterback should have a mental image of the location of *each* of his receivers *before* he completes the last of his backfield fakes. When he does, he has no problem picking up the offside end if his two primary receivers are covered.

Figure 3-4 illustrates another example of this technique, the "Double wing/Motion right/Cross fire counter at 5." Assume for the moment that the defense, a 5-2 monster, has been burned a few times too often by motion away from the monster. What does the defense do? Well, we know that they can rotate on backfield action in order to compensate to the side away from the monster. While they do it, they can also emphasize the need for penetration into the backfield in order to break up any of the offense's attempts at misdirection.

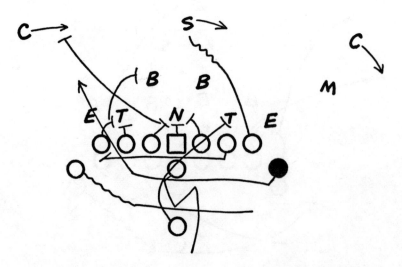

Figure 3-4 "Double Wing/Motion Right/XF Counter at 5"

Obviously, they are also banking on the fact that their multiple alignments and "let-it-all-hang-out" attack schemes are going to confuse the blocking assignments of the offense. Let's face it, sometimes they do. But if we keep them a dollar short and a day late throughout most of the game, their jitterbugging isn't going to rattle us.

Having the guts to call a good misdirection play on a well-sequenced play-action pass can do just that. Figure 3-4 shows one of our best counter plays out of the double wing, or, for that matter, out of almost *any* winged formation. It is particularly effective when the defense starts to prerotate with the motion as in figure 3-4.

PRINCIPLE NUMBER SIX: TRAP 'EM

The tackle trap gives us a dimension that has made our counter play one of our most effective offensive weapons. In conversation the other day with George Kelly, a coaching fixture at Notre Dame for almost twenty years and a former coach of mine at Nebraska, I asked what he considered to be the single most important principle he keeps in mind whenever playing an attack defense. He said, "That's easy—trap 'em."

I was inclined to agree, especially when I consider the past success of our counter plays. Against a reading defense, the tackle trap doesn't provide any obvious clues. As a matter of fact, the "triple double-team" on the noseman provides excellent strategy. Any well-coached linebacker is going to be reading *some kind* of a triangle. Middle linebackers in a six-man defensive front may read the two guards back to the fullback. Fifty-two linebackers may read the guard/fullback/quarterback combination, particularly against the double wing.

Regardless of what combinations they use, the guard is likely to be *one* of their keys—for obvious reasons. If the guard pulls or blocks down, he's invariably suggesting the direction of the play. Some teams may influence pull the guard, but rarely do they maintain a steady diet of such a strategy. So most good linebackers will key the guard and emphasize any one of several tactics to anticipate the play.

That's why we "triple double-team" the noseman. The tackle already is doing the pulling, and we're not giving up anything by way of penetration at the spot he's vacated because the fullback is filling for him. Once the linebackers see their guard block down on the noseman, what generally have they been instructed to do? Right—step up into the area vacated by the guard and expect some action.

That's just where we want them—as long as they don't get any penetration. To prevent their penetration, we instruct the tackle to make initial contact with his outside shoulder on the man on his head or slightly to his outside, then to release to the linebacker. The offensive right end is down-blocking his man anyway. The pulling tackle will clean up whatever is left.

At this point, the proponents of attack defenses get ego-involved and claim that a slanting line into their one or three "shades" will prevent the line from executing their assignments. If the line has a predetermined slant to their right—the offense's left—the offensive right tackle will have a hard time getting to the linebacker. Maybe, but at least he's going to be able to prevent penetration, and that's all we want. We don't need a devastating block because we've sucked the linebacker away from the point of attack already, and we've provided an angle for our right ends, irrespective of which way the defensive tackle is stunting. And if the defensive line is stunting to its left, so much the better.

We like the play, therefore, regardless of what the defense is doing. If it's reading, we've influenced it away from the point of attack. If it's precommitted to stunt, we've prevented its penetration. And we've turned one of our toughest blockers loose on a defensive player who is bound to be smaller than he is. It's fun to watch. An offensive tackle who gets to launch an armored attack on a smaller defensive end or outside backer works up a mighty big smile as he's galloping down the line of scrimmage.

As important, we have paved the way for several additional plays that complement the basic crossfire series, two of which have been unusually successful for us. Figure 3-5 illustrates the "Double wing/motion left/Cross fire counter at 6 pass." Once the counter play has picked up a few yards,

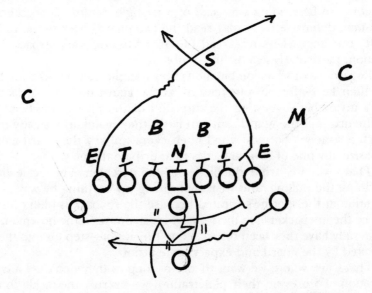

Figure 3-5 "Double Wing/Motion left/XF Counter at 6 pass"

we show the same action during a similar game situation, but this time we put the ball in the air, for a touchdown surprisingly often.

The play is identical to the counter at six in every way, with the single exception that the tackle doesn't pull. The line fires out, and the backs execute their fakes, concentrating on not showing pass too soon. The left end releases and stalks the safety just as he did on the running play. Once the safety reacts to him, the end breaks past him, angling toward the back flag in the end zone.

The right end makes preliminary contact with the man to his inside, holds for two full counts and then releases to the area vacated by the safety, who is likely to be chasing the left end. If he does a good job putting the safety to sleep, even getting him to react to the running action, the end can be *wide open* deep. We won a critical game one year with this play. The end was open by *twenty yards*.

If the saftey *does* manage to react to the left end, the right end is bound to be open somewhere in the middle just behind the hook zones. Both corners are already preoccupied, one with the motion, the other with the counterback coming down the line of scrimmage. That leaves the safety to cover both receivers, unless he gets some help from the monster man, who is likely to be too influenced by the counterback to react to the right end's two-count delay.

PRINCIPLE NUMBER SEVEN: ENTER THE SECONDARY WITH VARIABLE SPEED

In addition to the obvious advantages of a well-sequenced play-action pass, the play provides another, more subtle advantage. Recognizing the interrelated and mutually dependent responsibilities of defensive backs, any good passing team, particularly against attack defenses, capitalizes on the principles of variable speed and variable penetration into the secondary.

The counter-action pass is a perfect example. The left end is racing off the line of scrimmage, then stalking the safety. He then releases from his stalk on a deep angle toward the back flag. Just before he initiates his pass route, the right end is releasing from his two-count delay on the line of scrimmage.

The result is variable speed and penetration into the secondary. We like it for one big reason. During the early stages of any pass play, conventional or play-action, almost *any* potential receiver, unless he starts from a wide split, can enter almost *any* zone in the secondary. For this reason, defensive backs usually are instructed to be two steps deeper than the deepest potential receiver in or near their areas.

One receiver, therefore, in most zone coverages, can drive two men deep. Another delayed receiver, in this case the right end, generally can sneak into the secondary somewhere underneath the coverage, particularly in an attack defense with one or more linebackers abandoning the hook zones in order to blitz.

So we tell the quarterback to look for the left end first, because his reception is often for six points. If the left end is covered by the safety, the quarterback is to pick up the right end underneath. The timing generally is perfect, once we convince the left end to stalk and the right end to block for two counts. When the left end clears, the right end fills the area. It's a good play, particularly because all the quarterback has to do is watch the middle zone for coverage and timing.

Much more can be said about the execution of the play. It seems we never have enough time to refine all our plays to the point where they resemble the images we have of them. So we emphasize two important points, hoping that if *they* are accommodated, an occasional goof elsewhere won't compromise the play's chances for success.

The first point involves the faking, particularly the quarterback's. As with *any* play-action pass, he can't be in a big hurry. His movements must coordinate perfectly with the movements of the backs *and* the two ends. If the quarterback races through his backfield fakes, the ends will be wasting their time with their delays and won't be open soon enough to receive the quarterback's pass, which certainly will be rushed because he didn't take the needed time to deceive the defense.

Conversely, the backs won't have time to block and the ends will be given a message—loud and clear. By his actions, the quarterback will be telling the ends to get into their pass routes sooner—exactly what we *don't* want him to communicate. They'll execute only cursory stalks or delays, even to the point of bolting off the line like Carl Lewis out of the blocks. Once they start doing that, the quarterback will have to race through his fakes, and the whole play-action component will be lost.

A final word. Be sure to tell the wingback that his primary responsibility on the play is to block—not to fake. His initial movement down the line of scrimmage will be sufficient to influence the secondary, particularly if *our* line yells "counter!" There's nothing like helping the cause! The wingback doesn't need a clear mesh with the quarterback. Simply being in the immediate area will be sufficient. So we tell him to keep an eye on the outside pass rush. The harder the defensive end comes, the quicker the wingback has to come down the line of scrimmage to keep him off the quarterback.

Another play to run once the counter at six has worked a couple of times, particularly if the counter-action pass has been run with success, is the "T 7/Cross fire counter at 6/Screen right." Figure 3-6 illustrates how similar this play is to the running play and to the passing complement. But it capitalizes on a different component of the play action.

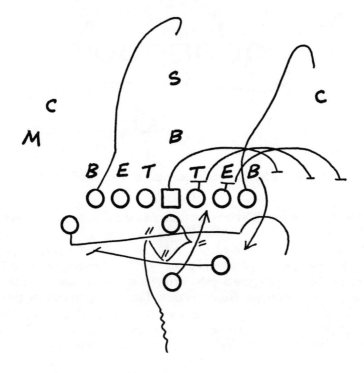

Figure 3-6 "T7/XF Counter at 6/Screen Right"

If the counter at six is even marginally sucessful and the counter-action pass at least gets the defense's attention once or twice, the defensive ends are likely to come hard, and the secondary is likely to disregard the wingback. Once they observe that he is a decoy and ostensibly not involved in the play action, they tend to forget about him in their haste to find the ball.

Then they are sitting ducks for a screen pass. That's one of our best reasons for throwing a screen pass to a counterback. He is often dismissed by the defense once they see that he doesn't have the ball. The defensive end, as a matter of fact, will do everything he can to avoid him once he senses pass. All the counterback has to do is lunge in the end's direction as if he's trying to make a block and then sneak in behind him.

An important element in the play is the counterback's technique. Obviously, he has to time his fakes so that he gets at least a small piece of the defensive end. Our quarterbacks are not so nifty that we can open the door to a good defensive end. Quarterbacks are too hard to find to have them running for their lives every time we throw a screen pass. So we instruct him to get down the line the way he normally would on a counter-action pass, then to give the onrushing lineman one good shot,

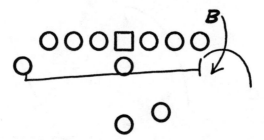

Figure 3-7 Screen right maneuver executed correctly

then let the man beat him *to the* outside and sneak out into the flat behind him.

If the back releases the rusher to his *inside,* the defender is going to sense screen, and the play will be over before it starts. Figure 3-7 illustrates the right way, figure 3-8 the wrong way. Emphasize the importance of the proper technique from *day* one. The kids, particularly those few who fail to grasp the big picture, are usually in too big a hurry to do it the right way. They are more anxious to get to the flat to catch the ball than they are to take the time to set up the end the way they are supposed to.

If they execute the proper technique, and the quarterback doesn't tip his hand too soon, the play is a gainer, often for big yardage. And it's not the last of the sequence. We also can call a screen pass to the motion back, even to the fullback—if we've been blessed with one who can catch the ball.

Figure 3-9 illustrates the "T 7/Cross fire counter at 6/Screen *left.*" On some occasions, particularly when we have a good one—and we usually do—the wingback may draw attention no matter where he goes or what he does. Many teams, including us, like to put one of their best athletes out on the wing.

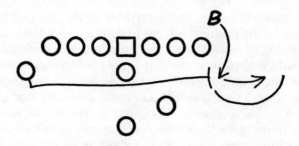

Figure 3-8 Executed incorrectly

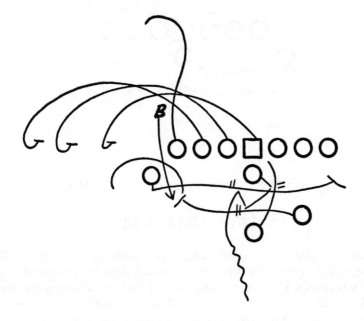

Figure 3-9 "T7/XF Counter at 6/Screen left"

Tom Osborne, the head coach of the Huskers, told me a couple years ago that he usually puts his best athlete on the wing. When one considers the running, blocking, and pass-receiving responsibilities of a good wing-back, it's not too surprising to see him draw a lot of attention. So we throw the ball to the motion man, as in figure 3-9.

USING THE FULLBACK

We also have one of our better players at the fullback position. The old truism that "you'd better run your fullback" has resulted in a wide variety of running plays for our fullbacks. We run with him and we throw to him, especially when we can sneak him out of the backfield with the "T 7/Cross fire counter at 6/*Middle* screen," as illustrated in figure 3-10.

This play is particularly effective versus attack defenses because we retain both backs for blocking purposes, and we have the opportunity to lose the fullback in the middle of the line. If the defensive linemen are penetrating and the linebacker(s) are coming, the fullback can be in excellent position to do some damage once he catches the ball. We can even set up a bogus screen to the outside if we want to decoy the action away from him.

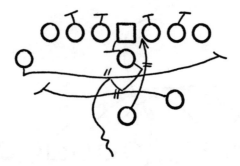

Figure 3-10 "T7/XF Counter at 6/Screen Middle"

LET'S WRAP IT UP

The point is that the double wing with motion gives us all kinds of offense, much more than the average attack defense can handle, particularly if it uses a monster man. We can run just about every play in our play book *without* giving away tendencies with our formation.

You can do much the same thing. Use your plays or incorporate some of ours into your offense. With just a modicum of imagination, the next game with your biggest rival can throw them for a loop when you line up in the double wing, and they have to decide what to do with their monster or which way to slant their line. It'll keep them off balance throughout most of the game, especially if you keep this chapter's principles somewhere in the back of your head.

One. Vary Your Offensive Sets. Remember that the double wing is not the only formation that upsets an attack defense. Oh, they will tell you that they have accommodated every possible variation in the offense's alignment—and they probably have. We tell everyone that we have. We use attack defenses, too. But we still get a little nervous when the opponent throws motion at us or shifts to his offensive variations before we get our heads on straight.

We also recognize that we are working with kids, whether they are fourteen or twenty-four, and we know that they enjoy predictability. Once different formations are thrown at them, they are forced to think, to adjust, to alter their mind sets. When the mind is engaged in sorting out adjustments, the body is a step slow and a split second late. At that point, we have the opponent beaten.

Figure 3-11 illustrates an unbalanced line that, in effect, retains a balanced offensive set. The line is unbalanced to the left, but the backfield set maintains a strong running threat to the right. The formation has 5 ½ men on either side of an imaginary line intersecting the center.

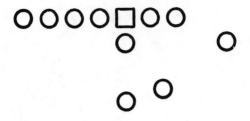

Figure 3-11

Figure 3-12 is unbalanced, too, but that same imaginary line reveals a total of 4 men on the right side of the center and 7 on the left. Obviously, the job of the offense is to determine the defense's adjustments to each formation. Any kind of standard defensive adjustment, such as sliding over a man, will affect what kinds of plays the offense calls.

The offense can get "real snappy" and shift to different backfield sets, adjust a tight end to create the imbalance, or motion into it. The thing to keep in mind, however, is that any defense, even an attack defense, doesn't like to alter its plans in mid-stream. Any variation of offensive alignment provokes them into something else—something they may not like.

In addition, it increases their chances to make a mistake. Remember the story of the boy who took a dollar to the bank to get ten dimes, then took the dimes to the drugstore for a dollar, then back to the bank for ten more dimes? He did this for an hour until a friend asked, "Why do you keep getting all those dimes?" The boy said, "Sooner or later, someone's gonna make a mistake, and it's not gonna be me."

Variable formations can give you the same edge.

Two. Trap 'Em. We illustrated the Trap 'Em principle with a counter play employing a tackle trap. Obviously, there are many others. We also like to short trap up the middle with our fullback, as in figure 3-13,

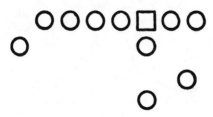

Figure 3-12

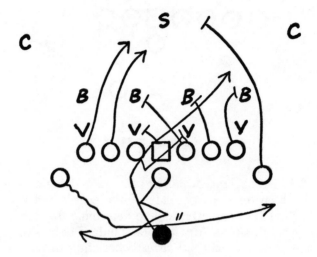

Figure 3-13 "XF 12 Trap"

because it gives us angles on most of the defensive linemen and backers, and the adjustments of the offense are minimal. Versus an even-man front, we tell the fullback to run more at zero, where the center used to be, in order to accommodate a possible defensive line slant into the gap between our center and right guard.

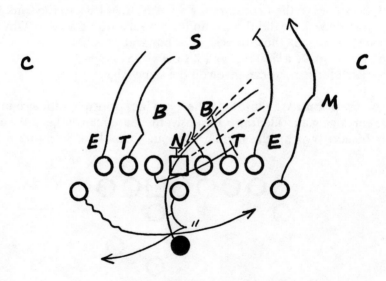

Figure 3-14 "XF 12 Trap

Versus an odd-man front, as in figure 3-14, we tell him to run his regular 12 action, which starts toward the one hole and angles back toward two, sometimes even four, depending on the defensive stunts. Within a matter of a few days after contact begins, our fullbacks always find the lane that almost always opens up between the dotted lines in the diagram. We designate the entire play a "T 8/Cross fire at 12 trap." It's always a big one for us.

We have a host of other trap plays, all of which complement one basic series. We'll diagram and discuss several as the book progresses. But now, the third principle from this chapter.

Three. Variable Speed and Penetration into the Secondary. Attack defenses usually do a good job covering their tails. Almost everyone in the front eight or nine has an attack angle and everyone in the secondary has a pursuit angle. Defenses will often just read, too, but when they are in the attack mode, they are particularly conscious of being sure the secondary covers definite pursuit lanes.

Any defense that remains in pure man-to-man coverage in the secondary is invariably asking for more than they can handle, so all defenses will vary their pass coverage but usually stick with some basic kind of

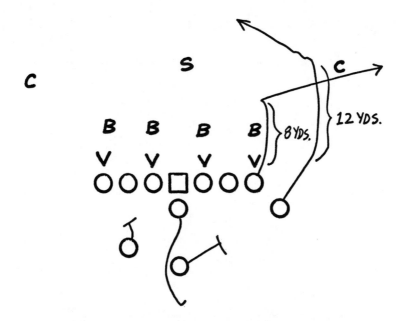

Figure 3-15 "T8/Dropback/Right Florida"

combination coverage. This is exactly what we want for our variable speed and penetration principle.

Everyone in the secondary has to be conscious of the deepest potential receiver in his zone. So, as in figure 3-15, which is a "T 8/Dropback-Right Florida," when the wingback runs a twelve-yard post at full speed and the right end runs an eight-yard flag at 3/4 speed, *someone* is in trouble. If the safety drops deep to anticipate the post coming into his zone, the end is likely to be open underneath the cornerback.

If the safety doesn't drop off but remains tight on the right end, the wingback's post is certain to get behind him, particularly because the left end's deep hook and slide is certain to hold the other cornerback.

We have many more pass plays that use this principle. As with everything else we have discussed so far, we will refer to it again, especially when we devote a future chapter to play-action passing.

But enough of the aerial attack. Let's get our feet back on the ground and take a good look at the battles going on in the trenches — where all the action is. Good line blocking is critical if the offense is going to be successful countering the attack.

4

Line Blocking Schemes and Techniques

Well, we can devise a myriad of strategies to combat the swarming techniques of most attack defenses, but when all is said and done the blocking of the line is the critical element in the offense's attempts to move the football. The backs are the glory boys and enjoy the cheers from the crowd and the ink from the press, but the linemen are the essential ingredient in the mix that makes a good football team. Without holes in the offensive line, even the most gifted back is just another tackling dummy searching for a little daylight and concentrating on his own survival.

When things are going according to the game plan and the backs are picking up touchdowns and high fives, they sometimes forget the hand-to-hand combat on the line that guaranteed the success of the latest offensive. The back who intermittently fakes or runs decoy routes doesn't experience the head-banging battles for supremacy that go on in the trenches.

Oh, don't get me wrong—I was a back and I coach the backs. We, too, receive our share of bumps and bruises. The periodic encounters we have with our fellow man smack more of *collision* than contact. Maybe that is the very reason we are so dependent on the line.

Perhaps the best way to describe the difference is to recount the story of a fullback we had a couple years ago who reluctantly made the transition to guard. It's a recurring threat for most fullbacks, and it became reality for this one. But he wanted to play football, so he made the switch.

After one week in his new position, he was asked how he liked it. Never at a loss for words, he said, "Fine." Seeking more of his scintillating

49

conversation, we asked him to describe the difference between being a back and a lineman. "It's a lot different," he said thoughtfully. "Linemen are bigger, tougher, and—sooner!"

His description was perfect, particularly for attack defenses, so the linemen require thoughtfully designed blocking schemes if they are to make holes in the defensive line. To get the job done unpredictably, we incorporate the backs into our blocking schemes. We use them from their home positions in the backfield, from the wing or slot positions, and with motion from the flanker spot. All those schemes, however, will be discussed in the next chapter, when we focus on the backs as blockers.

LINE BLOCKING STRATEGIES

We're not going to get fancy. That would be silly. Nor are we going to provide a total package that requires ten men and a chinese mathematician to figure out. A principle that has brought us considerable success up to this point is "keep it simple." We can so complicate our blocking schemes with unnecessary sophistication that even the National Merit Scholars on the team are bewildered. On occasion, in our desire to cover *all* the bases, we have done just that. The result has been confusion. And confused players lose.

Remember—when all is said and done, after we have waded through the verbiage of all those books out there, one simple fact remains. The team that makes the fewest mistakes usually wins. All else being *relatively* equal, the team that plays with its head and feels confident with the execution of its assignments is the team that is able to do the right thing at the right time.

Remember the soldier who said, "We have discovered the enemy— and it is us?" Well, we don't want to suddenly find ourselves in the enemy camp when we start brainstorming reasons why we may be losing the big ones. The kids are having enough trouble doing their jobs; they don't need us to throw a hundred different roles at them.

So, with that thought, let us recognize first of all that there are only so many different ways to block a hole. Obviously, we can block it straight; or we can cross block it. We can down block it, with either a trap or a kickout block from one of the backs. And we can finesse it—by *not* blocking one or more defensive men at the point of attack.

The fundamental principle involved is to use one of these schemes at the right time. We don't need a myriad of primary and secondary calls to get the job done. All we need is a few solid blocking schemes, and linemen smart enough to call them at the right time.

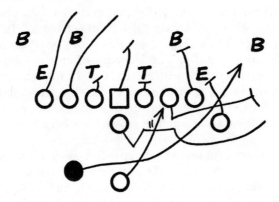

Figure 4-1

WHEEL IT

One of the principles we discussed earlier involved the ninth gap created by the Wing T. One of the reasons why it is so effective is illustrated in figures 4-1 and 4-2. The play call is "T 8/Inside belly at 6." It's basic within our offense, and characteristic of many Triple Option teams.

The quarterback rides the fullback into the four hole, who bellies away from the point of attack when the quarterback's ride is completed. The left halfback simulates with his first few steps an option path, then enters the six hole diagonally, receiving the ball from the quarterback on the line of scrimmage. The play is *most* effective, obviously, when we have had some success with the option pitch or run to the outside.

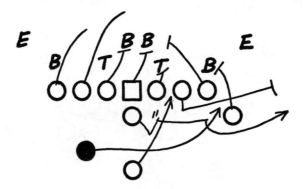

Figure 4-2

It is also effective when the tackle and end cross block at the six hole and, especially, when the tackle calls a "wheel block." Both diagrams illustrate the wheel block. Figure 4-1 shows the play versus a wide 4-4, figure 4-2 versus a split 4-4. The blocking scheme is solid, particularly against defenses that read the offensive ends. If, for example, the onside linebacker in figure 4-2 reads the end's down block and slides with him, he's only helping the wingback with *his* down block. Because few defenses read the tackle for trap action, the scheme has been very successful for us.

It is equally successful versus a defense like the 5-3 when the offensive tackle is covered. It doesn't make any difference to us which way the defense is stunting because each of the outside men has an angle on the player he is expected to block. Figure 4-3 illustrates the same play, an inside belly at 6, versus a 5-3. As you can see, the wheel block gives us an effective scheme. We can make it even more effective if we "Wheel and tackle finesse," as illustrated in Figure 4-4.

Given the nature of the inside belly action and the generalized responsibilities of defensive personnel, we can assume with some certainty that the defensive tackle will react to the fullback's fake, so often we won't bother to block him. This play has provided big yardage.

Take the whole thing one step further and complement the backfield action with a "T 8/inside belly at 4/right Delaware," as shown in figure 4-5. Every aspect of the play's execution is consistent with its running complement, the inside belly at 4, with the exception of the tackle pull.

The right end releases immediately to stalk the safety, and the wingback down blocks for two counts on the defensive end. Remember, most

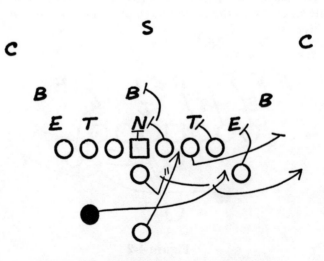

Figure 4-3 "T8/Inside belly at 6/Wheel"

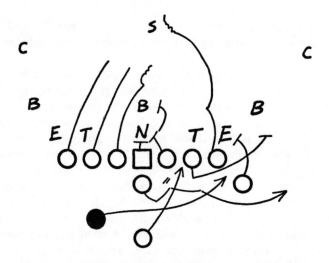

Figure 4-4 "T8/Inside belly at 6/Wheel finesse"

attack defenses instruct the defensive end and the outside backer to jam any inside release from the end or wingback. If the outside backer steps up to jam the wingback, he'll be clearly out of position when the wingback releases to the flat.

If the right end does a good job stalking the safety, he should have him flat-footed when he breaks for the flag. Because the cornerback is

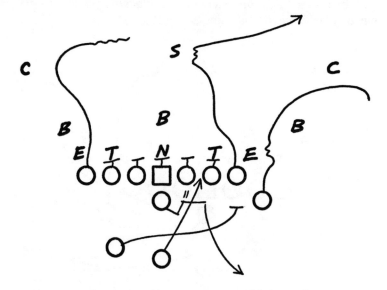

Figure 4-5 "T8/IB6/Right Delaware"

likely to be keying either the wingback and/or the end, he will be influenced to think run, particularly if the backs execute their fakes and the line fire-out blocks.

Someone is going to be open. Certainly, it isn't a sure bet because a lot of the time someone gets lazy and doesn't perform his requisite sell job. When everyone does his thing, however, the play is magic. And, most important, it doesn't have to be just *this* play to be magic. Any well-sequenced play-action pass, if sold properly, can do the same thing. All it takes is the very commonsensical notion that *no* defense, not even the best attack defense, can cover *everything* well; and well-conceived play-action passes give them more problems than they care to admit.

Finally, consider the problem posed by the "Inside belly option right/wheel-end finesse." The play is illustrated in figure 4-6 versus a wide 4-4 because it seems to be one of the most popular for "attack" enthusiasts. Generally, proponents of this defense assign the diveback—in this case the fullback—to the defensive end, the pitchback to the outside backer, and the quarterback to the inside backer.

A wheel block with an end finesse puts the wingback on the safety immediately and maintains the continuity with the play-action passing complement. It puts the right end immediately on the inside backer, and puts the outside backer in a no-win situation. If he takes the pitchback, which is usually his assigned responsibility, the quarterback keeps the ball—with the tackle as an additional blocker.

The Wing T, already a devastating offensive arrangement, can compound the problems of the defense by *not* blocking certain people, which brings us to our second blocking scheme.

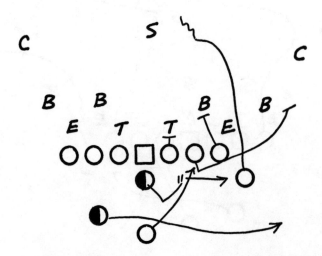

Figure 4-6 "T8/IB option at 8/Wheel finesse"

PRINCIPLE NUMBER EIGHT: DON'T BLOCK—FINESSE

The wide 4-4 currently is a very popular defensive alignment. It provides a highly diversified range of stunting alternatives, does a decent job defensing plays up the gut, and affords good containment to the outside. At least defensive coaches *think* it provides good containment.

Figure 4-7 illustrates the same inside belly option right, but with an end finesse. The offense obviously is making an assumption. We are assuming that the defensive assignments are consistent with those described in the previous section. Such an assumption seems warranted, however, because most defenses, attack or not, assign similar responsibilities. Even if our assumption is mistaken, we still can't go too far wrong finessing the defensive end. Our fullbacks are focal within our running offense, so they invariably attract a lot of attention.

If the fullback executes a good fake—from inside belly *or* veer action— the defensive end will almost certainly be influenced to the inside. Most important, by *not* blocking him, we're able to release the offensive end to the inside backer and to put the wingback on the cornerback. Because the offensive right tackle is free to go immediately to the safety, the play has everyone blocked by the time the quarterback makes his move upfield. Regardless of what attack devotees claim, the pursuit paths of the offside defenders will not get them close enough to the quarterback to prevent a good gainer.

So you say "Big deal; most good triple option teams have been doing that for a long time now." We agree, and so have other teams. Good

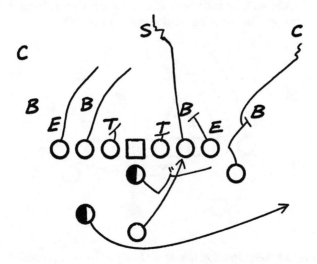

Figure 4-7 "T8/IB option at 8/Finesse"

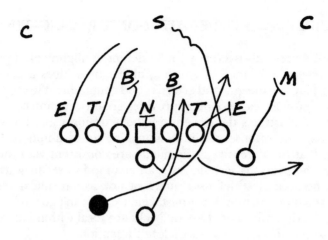

Figure 4-8

"veer" teams will finesse one or more defensive players. But *one* point is that a good finesse doesn't have to be restricted to an option play. Figure 4-8 illustrates a "T 8/Inside belly at 6/tackle finesse."

If the fullback ride is well executed, the tackle will react to him, *whether or not* he is on a predetermined stunt. So we don't block him. Besides, if he remains unblocked, he is likely to look for a trap or a lead block from one of the backs, so he is *likely* to react to the fullback.

The defensive end is likely to be hand-playing the offensive right end, who is trying to fight past him to get to the safety. By the time the end clears, the tackle will be initiating his block on the defensive end and the ball carrier will be arriving at the point of attack.

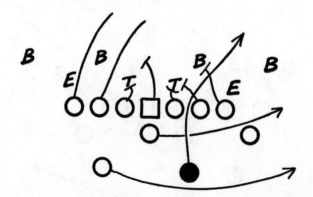

Figure 4-9 "Pro/Quick at 4/Double finesse outside"

The timing is just about right. It is also excellent when we "double finesse" the outside. Consider again the wide 4-4 and a simple line play. As illustrated in figure 4-9, we call it a "Pro 8/Quick at 4/Double Finesse Outside." The play is one of football's oldest—and best.

THE OLD-FASHIONED WAY

Let's admit it. Our offense is as sophisticated as anyone's. We can come at you with hundreds of variations on our basic series, but when all is said and done, we still rely heavily on good, old-fashioned football. All those prolific imaginations out there have provided us with a smorgasbord of offensive football; but good old bread and butter still gets the job done. It may not be as exciting to the sophisticated palate, but it's every bit as satisfying when it puts points on the scoreboard.

So we call the "Quick at 4" with some regularity, primarily because we can complement it with a quick-hitting counter play, an option very similar to the veer, and a variety of play-action passes, many of which will be described in chapter ten. As important, the double finesse block on the outside, as illustrated versus a wide 4-4, gives us as strong a blocking scheme as ever was developed against *any* attack defense.

Obviously, it's most effective when the offensive tackle is uncovered and has two defenders to his outside, as with the split 4-4 in figure 4-10. But it's equally effective versus attack defenses that run predominantly from a 5-2 set, as in figure 4-11. All we do is run the play tighter, at the 2 hole.

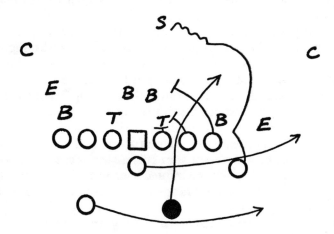

Figure 4-10 "Pro 8/Quick at 4/Double out finesse"

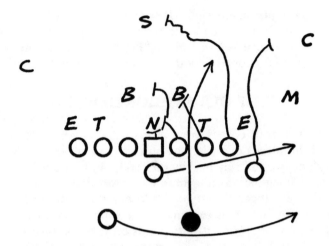

Figure 4-11 "Pro 8/Quick at 4/Double out finesse"

The inside-release is the key. The defensive player isn't alive who can try to make contact with the man on his head and still catch a halfback diving to his inside. He may on a rare occasion get a hand on the back, but a slap never dropped even a moderately good running back. And versus a 5-2 defense, when the defensive tackles are usually aligned on their outside, the *un*blocking scheme is even more effective.

It is particularly effective against a strong and mobile noseguard who picks a side without apparent rhyme or reason. The double finesse on the outside enables us to double team the noseguard or to plateau to the offside linebacker if the noseman stunts away.

The principle of finessing defensive linemen is not restricted to the outside. As hard as it may be for you to accept it, it works. Figure 4-12 illustrates a "T 7/Cross fire at 2/Tackle off finesse." The "tackle off" refers to the offside tackle, and it simply instructs the left guard to inside-release to the linebacker. As illustrated, the blocking scheme is excellent versus the split 6. It's just as effective versus the 4-4 stack.

The point is, finesse blocking can be used anywhere along the line of scrimmage and will provide for you a surprisingly effective line blocking strategy. Take a quick review of your current series and reevaluate your blocking strategies. We will guarantee that *somewhere*, probably quite often, you will be able to use finesse techniques as alternatives to what you are doing currently.

We have a wide variety of additional blocking strategies, all of which help us get the job done. Like you, we cross block and double cross block in the middle of the line. Versus the Pro 4-4/Split 6 alignment, we'll attack the middle with a double cross scheme as illustrated in figure 4-13.

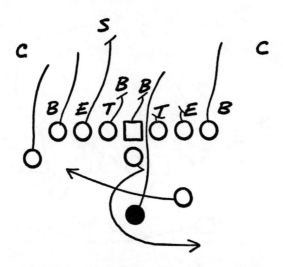

Figure 4-12 "T7/XF at 2/Tackle off finesse"

All we instruct the fullback to do is get additional depth and run to daylight. The scheme is effective when the tackles jam and the linebackers read. It is even more effective when the tackles jam and the linebackers scrape on a predetermined stunt to the outside—either side. It makes no difference.

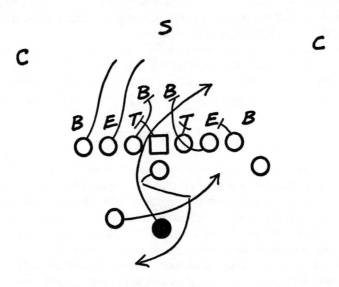

Figure 4-13 "T8/XF at 1/Double cross"

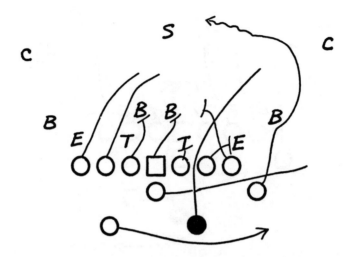

Figure 4-14 "Pro 8/Quick at 4/Exit"

Cross blocking is also the key for another of our basic plays, our Quick at 4.

Figure 4-14 illustrates a "Pro 8/Quick at 4/Exit Block" versus a split 4-4. The blocking scheme is a natural because of the angles it provides. The term "Exit" is an acronym for "End Crosses Inside Tackle." It simply instructs the tackle to go first and the end to cross after him to block anything to show to the inside, in this case probably the onside linebacker. Again, as with all the other schemes, unless predetermined in the huddle, the tackle will call the blocking scheme.

There are a variety of other defenses against which the scheme is effective. The point is that we can get a lot of mileage out of our tackles if we use them intelligently. That's another reason we trap with the tackles with all our counter plays. They perform well—and they like it.

LET'S WRAP IT UP

Well, it is no startling revelation to say that any blocking scheme, no matter how basic or how sophisticated, must be called at the right time to be effective. It also must be executed well. On occasion we will call the scheme on the sidelines when we anticipate a certain defensive set. Usually, however, the linemen will call the strategy on the line of scrimmage. All they look for is an angle with each block.

The schemes, as indicated earlier, are not shockingly different from what most teams do, but they do work very well against attack defenses because they seek angles wherever possible and capitalize on trapping possibilities. Anything too shockingly different is always suspect in my mind anyway. Our goal is to seek out the tried and true, invest it with an innovative wrinkle or two, and use it against what enthusiasts of attack defenses consider unbeatable strategies.

The *worst* thing we can do is allow attack defenses to push us into unfamiliar territory—in essence, to overreact. Once our passions get the best of us, we are like sailors putting to sea in a storm. Let's keep the waters calm by recognizing first that attack defenses are not that earth-shaking in design and, second, that we can beat them by keeping in mind a few simple principles.

Another of those principles involves using the backs a bit differently—the focus of the next chapter.

5

Leading the Way: Backs as Blockers

Question: what brings more joy to a coach's heart than having a kinesthetic genius in the backfield who can elude tacklers the way the Artful Dodger avoided cops? Answer: ten blockers who can open holes for him. Even when the runner has only moderate ball-carrying skills, we get a lot of mileage out of our running game when the other ten players are good at knocking people down.

If our reputations as coaches were contingent upon our developing gifted kinesthetic runners, we'd all be in a lot of trouble—by definition. Gifted kinesthetic runners are just that. They are blessed with the inborn ability to sense daylight and to translate that sense into a physical grace that reflects the natural harmony of their bodies. All we as coaches have to do is devise strategies that get the ball to them as often as possible.

Then we make sure we do something about the blockers. We can develop *them*. Great runners are born; great blockers are *made*. Occasionally we will be fortunate enough to find both in a single player. But if a kid doesn't have the natural moves of a great runner, his desire to play the game can make him a great blocker. Great runners may be the arms and legs of a solid football team, but great blockers are its heart. The runners provide excitement, but the blockers provide stability as well as the intensity needed for consistently winning efforts.

So we work long and hard to make blockers of all our backs. Fortunately, it is not a very difficult task. We have experienced so much success within the past ten years that our winning tradition imposes expectations on the kids they might not otherwise experience *anywhere*. They are expected to dig deep and to push for a maximum effort at all times.

If a kid can make that commitment, he can be a blocker. He doesn't have to be big. If he varies his blocking techniques based on the game circumstances, and uses his brain as well as his head, he can handle any defensive player, regardless of his size.

CONFIDENCE BUILDERS

A case in point involves a drill the backs used to love. Once we began to feel comfortable with our pass blocking techniques, we'd send our smallest back to where the linemen were practicing and challenge them to try to get to our quarterback. Early in the season the linemen jumped at the chance to dish out generous slices of humble pie.

That isn't the way it worked out. Every time the linemen rushed hard, the backs dropped and blocked through their knees. Then, when the linemen started feeling their way, the backs stung them with a good head and shoulder block. All the backs had to do was vary the technique. After a couple such challenges, the linemen decided not to take us up on our offer any more. They had already developed a healthy respect for the backs as blockers, and the coaches had decided that the potential for knee injuries was too great to continue the drill.

Such a blocking strategy is one reason that some states, particularly in high school, have outlawed any blocking below the waist outside the "clip zone." Their intent is to save knees. Maybe it isn't a bad idea. Regardless of the merits of the rule, let's simply recognize that any kind of variable blocking strategy is going to do the job better than just one.

So, depending on the play and the situation, we will instruct our players to use one of several techniques: crab, drive, or shield block. We are unable to chop block anymore because of the prohibitions in our state rules. But we still crab after initial contact, and, obviously, we drive and shield block.

As a matter of fact, we probably shield block more than most teams. It is an extremely effective block downfield because players can sustain it longer than any other block. We will discuss it in a future chapter because it has a strong relationship to our play-action passing component.

The block we will emphasize in this chapter is the straight shoulder or, as we call it, drive block. It is identical to the iso block used so successfully by Notre Dame for so many years. The back is assigned a man on defense, generally a linebacker or a safety, and he is instructed to drive block him away from the point of attack.

We can't use the chop block because the rules prohibit it. We wouldn't use it anyway because it just doesn't get the job done against attack defenses. Too often, our fullbacks have angled through the line for an iso block on the middle linebacker and have opted to chop him instead of bringing him to a standstill with a solid shoulder block. Too often, we've seen the middle linebacker still make the tackle by diving over the blocker or by simply side-stepping him.

If the middle linebacker is a fire-breather with Dick Butkus's temperament, we may be forced occasionally to go to his knees. But if a team has a middle linebacker like that, they don't need to attack on defense very often, so our offense will emphasize deception and will rely less on backs leading the play through the hole.

PRINCIPLE NUMBER NINE: BLOCK WITH BACKS AND USE MORE DOUBLE TEAMS.

Figure 5-1 illustrates a full house formation and what we call a "Crossfire at 4 lead." It is diagrammed against a split 6 because it is so popular with many teams as a good defensive variation. First of all, notice how the fullback's fake at one helps to hold both linebackers if they are reading. If they aren't, it makes little difference to us because the blocking scheme is solid enough to handle any defensive stunt.

Our rule simply instructs the back to block the first linebacker or safety *at the point of attack or to his inside.* Whenever the line hears "lead," they know that the linebacker nearest the point of attack is to be blocked by the back, so, if uncovered, they will always down block. Obviously, versus a split 6, the onside linebacker is nearest the point of attack, so he becomes the responsibility of the lead blocker.

Versus a 5-2, as evidenced in figure 5-2, the left linebacker is nearest the point of attack, so the offensive onside guard, because he is uncovered, will end up double-teaming the noseman with the center. This, too, has obvious advantages. If the defense is in a predetermined scrape, as illustrated in figure 5-3, the lead back can bypass the scraping linebacker, look to the inside for the offside backer adjusting, or go right

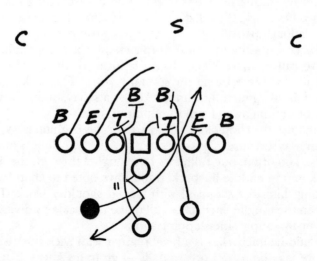

Figure 5-1 "Full house/XF 4 lead"

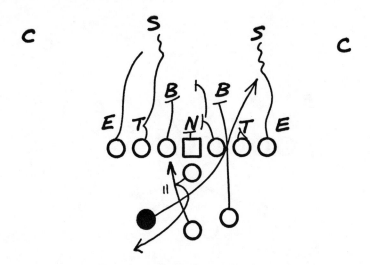

Figure 5-2

to the safety. The blocking scheme has the capability of transforming defensive maneuvers into clear disadvantages.

Figure 5-4 illustrates the point further, the same play, a crossfire at four lead, versus a wide 4-4. The play may not be quite as successful because of the untouched outside backer, but his outside responsibility should preoccupy him initially. Even if he does get in on the tackle, the play is still good for a five- or six-yard gain, because the offensive tackle's down-block results in a double team on the defensive tackle, which the runner has been instructed to favor.

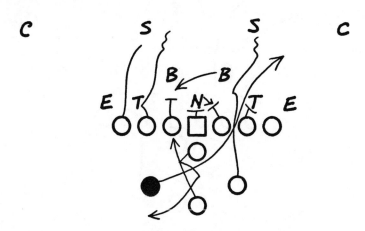

Figure 5-3

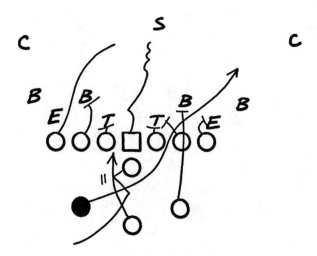

Figure 5-4

The rule is consistent against any defense and provides a solid blocking scheme against any attack defense, even an occasional overload at the point of attack. It also gives us an excellent bootleg pass out of the full house formation. With the exact same backfield action, we are able to execute a pass play that not only puts the usual pressure on the outside defensive personnel but places the safety in a three-deep secondary in a no-win situation.

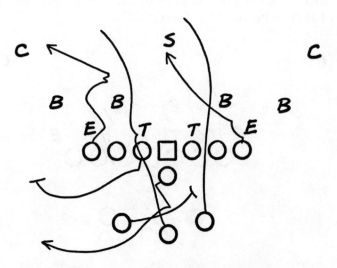

Figure 5-5 "XF bootleg pass at 7"

Figure 5-5 illustrates a "Cross fire at 4 lead/bootleg pass at 7." As evidenced by the diagram, it is the perfect complement to the running play and gives us four potential receivers in an area covered by a maximum of three defenders. There is no need for us to go into the specifics of its execution because we will be doing that in a later chapter. For now, let us just recognize that "complementarity" is the key. Everything has to look like everything else.

OTHER SERIES

Now that the lead concept has been introduced, let's look at additional examples of its use from series other than crossfire action. The inside belly has always been a good series for us, particularly versus "reading" linebackers. Our program has embraced the principle for years that an offense is successful only if it runs its fullback. We don't want a 230-pound unidirectional hulk who has the kinesthetic sense of a stampeding buffalo.

If *occasionally* he can be a stampeding buffalo, we won't complain, but generally we prefer a solid ball carrier with the ability to run to daylight. That's why we will vary our inside belly attack to include the "T 7 motion/ Inside belly at 4 lead," as illustrated in figure 5-6. Obviously, we can run it without motion to assure the purity of a weakside attack, and often we will.

The point is, we like to put a good, blocking halfback on a linebacker. It strengthens our line blocking scheme and diversifies our play-action

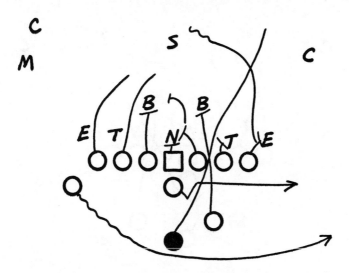

Figure 5-6 "T7 Motion/Inside belly at 4 lead"

passing attack. Let's remember throughout this chapter that the block doesn't have to be devastating. A good shield block is often as effective as anything else. Much of the time, all the blocker has to do is keep his body between the linebacker and the ball carrier. A good ball carrier can do the rest. So can a good blocker.

Generally, however, a back with pride is going to sting the linebacker. In so doing, he will establish the strength of play-action. He also will engender a little anxiety in even the hardest hitter. Linebackers enjoy the general security of being involved in a protected situation. Defensive linemen are instructed to "hit the man in front of them" to keep immediate blockers off the linebackers. Linebackers certainly receive their share of "blind-side" blocks, one reason why their knees grind like universal joints once they hit middle age.

But, generally, they are well protected by linemen who are *expected* to bang heads on every play and to protect their piece of turf by firing out low and making contact with the man in front of them. If all that is done effectively, they should free up the linebackers to make most of the tackles.

Linebackers, then, really don't expect to get hit very often. Oh, they have to react off a pile, or step up and meet a hard-charging lineman at the point of attack, but they generally don't expect any *collisions* until *they* initiate them when they make a tackle.

That is why they don't like halfback or fullback lead blocks. Early in the game, they don't *expect* to be blocked by a back leading through the hole. They expect to see halfbacks faking or running the ball, or releasing

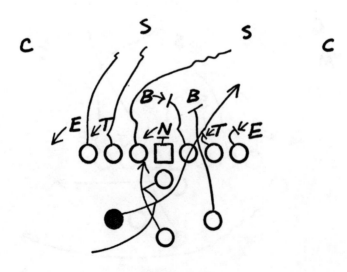

Figure 5-7

for passes, not blocking. Fullbacks pound through the line in search of linebackers, but halfbacks usually don't do anything that will purposely dirty their uniforms.

They do on our team; and they make believers of linebackers, particularly linebackers who sit four to five yards off the line of scrimmage to get a good look at their keys. Figure 5-7 illustrates a 5-2 defense that scrapes its linebackers and slants its line charge, sometimes randomly but generally into the strength of the formation. The play call is "Full house/Inside belly at 4 lead."

Again, the right halfback is assigned an iso block on the onside linebacker, freeing up the right guard to two-team the noseman. If the line slant is in the opposite direction, the right guard is instructed to go the next plateau, which would be the offside linebacker. The right tackle is taking a position step to the inside to seal the gap, so it makes little difference which way the defensive tackle is slanting.

If the safety is instructed to invert in order to get his nose into the action sooner, we like to call the "Full house/Inside belly at 4/lead-follow," as illustrated in figure 5-8. Now, we get the fullback into the blocking action. Even if the quarterback is only a mediocre runner, the play is a ground-gainer, especially if the quarterback favors the two-team block on the noseman. Remember, the lead block provides an automatic two-team block on a stunting noseman, and when that happens, a defense that scrapes its inside linebackers is in trouble.

If the noseman slants to his right, our right guard simply plateaus to the scraping linebacker. If the noseman slants to his left, he runs right

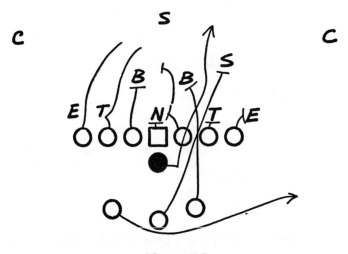

Figure 5-8

into the two-team block; and the linebacker, if his scrape is predetermined, runs himself out of the play. The lead block concept, therefore, not only puts a good-blocking halfback on a linebacker, but it frees up a lineman to increase the blocking strategies at the point of attack. Which of the two is more important, we don't know. But we like them both. They work.

FOLLOWING TO DAYLIGHT

Here's one that works well, too. Figure 5-9 illustrates a "T 8/Cross fire at 1/Quarterback follow." In essence, the play involves a lead block by the fullback on the linebacker and a keep by the quarterback at the one hole. The play is excellent for us because we run a lot of cross fire action, so much that the linebackers in a 5-2 cross-key our backs.

So we turn their keys into an advantage. The offside linebacker is going to stay at home because our left halfback is moving in his direction. If the fullback makes a lousy fake, the onside backer will look elsewhere for the play. In essence, the poor fake will set up the linebacker for a better block.

All the quarterback does is fake to the fullback, take one step toward the left half, flash the ball in front of him, and drive off his back leg into the one hole. The play is very successful for us. Again, the fullback lead gives us the same line blocking advantages against the slanting noseman and scraping linebackers.

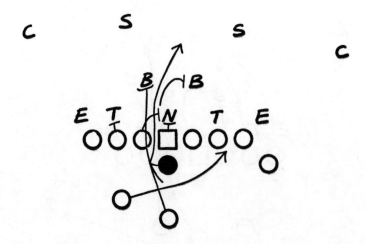

Figure 5-9 "T8/XF1/Quarterback follow"

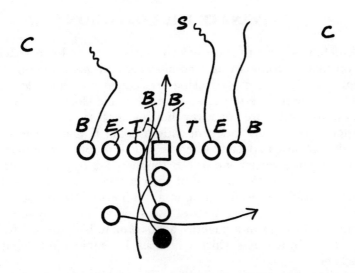

Figure 5-10 "I left/Power at 1/FB lead"

This also happens in our I formation with power action. Figure 5-10 illustrates an "I left/Power at 1/FB lead." This time, we are illustrating it against a split 6 or a split 6 look. We have already determined its effectiveness against the 5-2. It is important to realize that the blocking rules are just as consistent with other defenses. The lead blocker still picks up the onside linebacker, and the linemen at the point of attack block off if uncovered.

The play gives us the same advantages as the other "lead" plays. It puts a good blocking back on a linebacker and, as important, it frees up a lineman to double team a defensive lineman. This latter point is really significant. Why do defenses tandem? Obviously, the primary reason is to confuse blocking schemes. In the 6-2 illustrated in figure 5-10, they hope to confuse the offense's blocking schemes by sending the tackle into the center gap on one play and the linebacker into it the next. The strategy, a fundamental principle of most attack defenses, is a good one and usually works.

But we don't care *which way* the tandem stunts. Our double-team block on the onside defensive tackle takes all the guesswork out of the blocking scheme. If the tackle slants into the center/guard gap, we double-team him. If he slants into the center/guard gap, our left guard takes him alone, and the center plateaus to the linebacker. The added bonus of plateauing to the linebacker is that it frees up our fullback to continue downfield for the safety or to clean up on either linebacker.

ELIMINATE THE CONFUSION

Attack defenses want to confuse you. They want to force you into a situation that confounds your line blocking and gives them a straight shot into your backfield. By freeing up a lineman with the lead block, we don't let them. In essence, we establish a line blocking scheme that doesn't particularly care *which* way they go, because our responsibilities are determined largely independently of what *they* intend to do. We know what we have to do, and when we do it, our opponent is in trouble.

A recent game versus one of our toughest 5-2 opponents serves to illustrate. They like to blitz one of their safeties and scrape with the linebackers inside. So we lined up in a full house formation to present a balanced offensive look. Because we showed no strongside to our formation, they were in a quandry as to *where* to blitz the safety. They also were forced to guess which way to slant the line and to scrape the linebackers.

However, the *important* point is that we didn't care *which* way they stunted. We even were able to predict more often than they liked which way they would slant the line charge because they opted to go to the wide side of the field, the only real choice they were sure of. We *did* care about the safety blitz, but once he started tipping his hand, a simple "over" call by our quarterback transformed a "Cross fire at 4 lead" into a "Cross fire at *3* lead." The balanced backfield set gave us that option, too.

We beat them—one of our toughest opponents, an outstanding program—by twenty-some points. After the game, their head coach was very gracious in defeat. He really *did* have a tough time stopping the "lead" block and the double-teaming it provides on the line.

HAMMER THE OUTSIDE MAN

We double-teamed not only the noseman but the defensive tackle as well. As a sequenced alternative to the "Cross fire at 4 lead," we called a "Full house/Cross fire at 6 hammer." The hammer block uses the blocking skills of the halfback, too, but it instructs him to block the outside man on the defensive line instead of the onside linebacker. See figure 5-11.

The double-team block still occurs to the inside of the back's block, this time on the defensive tackle. The center seals onside, and the right guard blocks the onside linebacker, unless a predetermined stunt scrapes him out of the play, in which case he moves directly toward the safety. The right end does fundamentally what the right guard did using the Cross fire at 4 lead. He two-teams the tackle, unless the tackle slants across the face of our offensive tackle. If the defensive tackle slants

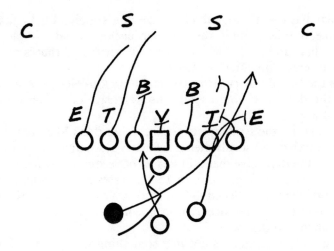

Figure 5-11

away—toward the tackle-guard gap—the end is instructed to plateau to the linebacker or, if he is scraping away, the safety.

The play gives us the same advantages as the lead block. First, it puts a solid blocker on the outside man on the defensive line. Second, it gives us a double-team block at the point of attack with the option to plateau if the defensive man slants away.

We *can* use the blocking scheme with other series as well, as illustrated in figure 5-12. The play call is "Full house/Inside belly at 6 hammer."

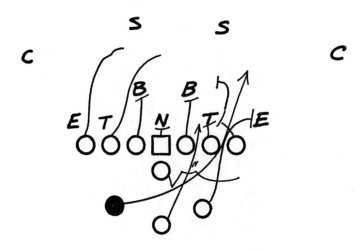

Figure 5-12 "Full house/IB6 hammer"

This play has the additional advantage of a sustained belly fake at the four hole, but the point is, the hammer block is a solid six-hole blocking scheme that can be used with any of your series and that is consistently effective versus any attack defense.

So is the "bend" block. It instructs the back to block the second man in on the defensive line, usually the defensive end, hence the name bend—Back on *END*.

We don't use the strategy often because we don't like to ask our half-backs to survive on a steady diet of regularly blocking perhaps the biggest player on the defensive team. But as an occasional variation on the lead block, you can't beat it. Figure 5-13 illustrates a "Full house/Cross fire at 4/Bend" versus a stacked 4-4. It instructs our offensive right end to outside-release on the backer, who normally will assume containment responsibility on that side.

If the outside tandem is dealing, something they usually don't want to do, we simply let the end block the defensive end, and we tell the lead back to block the linebacker coming to the inside. Again, the double team block on the defensive tackle gives us a sure bet if he is jamming the guard/tackle gap and the backer is stunting toward the center. If the defensive tackle is stunting *away*, toward the guard/center gap, we tell our tackle to plateau to the linebacker who probably will be coming. All he does, as with all the double-team blocks, is take a lead step toward the lineman and adjust his path if the lineman is slanting away.

Again, we don't use a steady diet of this strategy. All we need, however, is once or twice a game to keep the tackle guessing. And usually, each time the back bend blocks him, the tackle is completely surprised. Com-

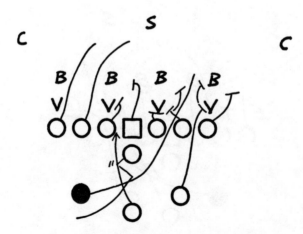

Figure 5-13 "Full house/XF4 bend"

bine that strategy with the lead block and an occasional trap block and the defensive tackle is a basket case by the end of the game·

HIT WITH A WHAM

Another strategy that frustrates the linemen is our wham play. Figure 5-14 illustrates an "I right/Wham at 4." Obviously, it's a short-yardage play that provides three double-team blocks at the point of attack. There have been instances, however, when attack defenses have forced us to make a steady diet of the wham formation and its play variations.

For example, once the linebackers start submarining or cheating up, we will line up in the I right—our wham formation—give the defense the tendency by formation, and then run a "Power right/hammer," as shown in figure 5-15. Again, the halfback hammers the outside man on the line of scrimmage, and now we have the fullback leading the tailback through the hole.

Then, when the team adjusts its defense with something like a tandem stack to the weak side of the formation with the noseman offset to strength, we'll run an "I right/Cross fire QB keep at 7," as illustrated in figure 5-16. The principle, again, is "keep 'em guessing." Show one thing; do another. Establish as many double-team blocks on the line of scrimmage as possible by using backs as blockers. The strategy provides power and enables the linemen to adjust easily by plateauing.

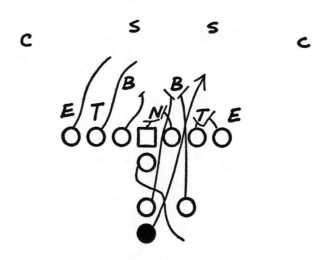

Figure 5-14 "I Right/Wham 4"

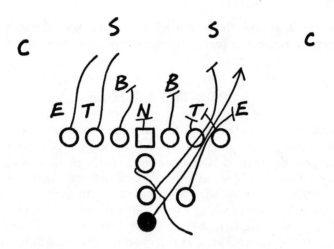

Figure 5-15 "I Right/Power Right hammer"

A final example of using backs as blockers involves the wingback trap. Figure 5-17 illustrates a "T 8/Cross fire at 6/Wingback trap." The blocking scheme is not particularly unique, but it does provide the occasional variation we require to drive a defensive tackle out of his mind. It is a variation of the bend block, only it's a little sneakier. It is very effective once or twice a game, and its use is restricted only by the creativity of the coach who uses it.

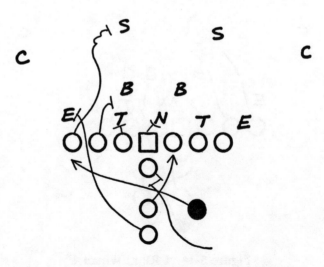

Figure 5-16 "I Right/XF QB keep at 7"

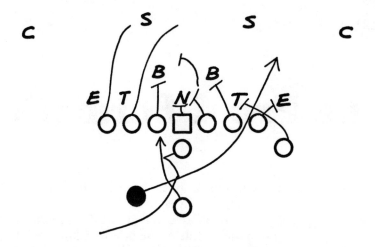

Figure 5-17 "T8/XF6/Wingback trap"

LET'S WRAP IT UP

We like this chapter. The concept of using a back as a blocker and freeing up a lineman to help two-team or plateau to a linebacker has brought us a great deal of success against some very solid attack defenses. Obviously, we are sold on the idea. It transforms the purported strength of stunting defenses—their unpredictable charges—into harmless movements that play right into the hands of the offense's blocking schemes.

The lead concept, for example, neutralizes the tactics of even the most skilled noseman and virtually eliminates the strategic effectiveness of any kind of inside scrape maneuver. The hammer block, the bend block, and the wingback trap simply provide variations on the main theme. They launch a surprise attack on one of the defensive players and enable the linemen to double-team *someone* or to plateau block at the point of attack.

As evidenced in some of the illustrations, particularly early in the chapter, the strategy also provides for some interesting and generally very effective play-action passing complements. Obviously, there are more. Chapter 10, however, is devoted exclusively to the passing component, so we will wait till then to discuss further examples of play-action passes.

The principle of using backs as blockers has provoked additional elements in our offensive strategizing. It has given use to a special formation that combines elements of two principles: backs as blockers and provoking an offensive overload at the point of attack. We call it the Pro 4 Special. It will be the focus of the next chapter.

6

The Pro 4 Formation

Well, let's resurrect one of our original arguments for using the Wing T versus attack defenses. Against any eight-man defensive set, regardless of the alignment, it offers one more gap than the defense can cover. If we squeeze that gap into the middle of the offensive line, we introduce a formation that provides for an obvious overload at the point of attack and that can chase the most steadfast attack defense into a different alignment, one that it may not be as prepared to play.

PRINCIPLE NUMBER TEN: OVERLOAD THE
POINT OF ATTACK

Figure 6-1 illustrates the Pro 4 set against a 5-2 alignment. You can imagine it against *any* attack alignment. The *important* thing is to imagine just what your offense will enable you to do with it. The extra blocker between the guard and tackle provides for all kinds of possibilities. And remember: he might be one of your best blocking backs, or he could be your third guard wearing a back's number.

If you have a good ball carrier who is also a good blocker, the diversity he brings to the position will be unbeatable. If you don't have such a player, use a guard on every play or intermittently, as the needs of the game dictate.

The important element of the formation, however, is that you have an excellent overload in the middle of the line that provides more blocking power than the average attack defense can handle. It also provides an excellent way to handle the linebacker, regardless of the exact defensive alignment, who comes up close to the line of scrimmage and tries to sneak his way through the center/guard or guard/tackle gaps.

Any normal "home" backfield alignment will be unable to get to the line of scrimmage quickly enough to intercept the linebacker and to keep him out of the play. With the Pro 4 alignment, however, and any of the other three or four similar alignments in our bag of strategic tricks, we have a blocking back close enough to the line of scrimmage to be able to pick up the linebacker.

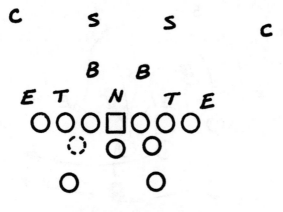

Figure 6-1 "Pro 4"- 3

During the past several years, we have found it necessary to go into our slot 3 and 4 alignments often during the season. The need has become evident because attack defenses, particularly the eight and nine-man fronts, like to penetrate into the backfield to confuse blocking schemes and to disrupt any kind of simple misdirection or counter action.

The Pro 4 gives us exactly what we need to be able to pick up that additional blitzer, no matter how close he is to the line of scrimmage. In essence, then, the Pro 3 and Pro 4 offensive alignments, and the Wing 3 and Wing 4, which will be described in a subsequent chapter, borrow a page from the books of all those attack-defense coaches. They overload the point of attack and create a situation that most defensive alignments are unable to handle.

As with the "full house lead" concept, we don't have to spend an awful lot of time trying to figure out exactly who we're going to block because the overload at the point of attack provides a one-on-one blocking situation that's more predictable and a double-team block somewhere along the line of scrimmage, usually right *at* the point of attack.

IMMEDIATE BLOCKING

Consider figure 6-2, which illustrates the Pro 4 alignment with a "Quick at 4" versus a 5-2 defensive front. As with the "Cross fire at 4 lead," which was discussed in the previous chapter, the alignment of our backfield personnel gives us an immediate block from the four-back on the onside linebacker and provides a double-team block on the noseman. Again, if the noseman stunts away, the right guard will plateau to the offside linebacker who may or may not be scraping into our point of attack.

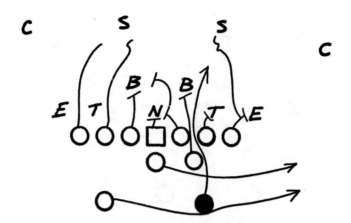

Figure 6-2 "Pro 4/Quick at 4"

If the noseman stunts *toward* the offensive right guard, the guard will double team with the center, and the four-back will go right at the linebacker, who may or may not be scraping *away* from our point of attack. If he scrapes away from the point of attack, the setback will continue his path directly toward the safety, looking to the inside for the other linebacker, who may have been cross-keying.

Notice that the play can be equally effective versus a six-man defensive front, in the case of figure 6-3, a split 6. Because the split 6 tries to take away much of your inside game by jamming the down tackles into the

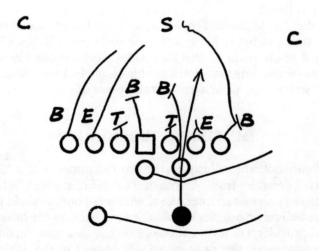

Figure 6-3 "Pro 4/Quick at 4"

gaps between the center and offensive guards, they tend to use some of their biggest and toughest players in those positions.

The Pro 4 alignment enables us to take him in the direction he wants to go, to put the center on the offside linebacker, and to send the setback directly to the onside linebacker, who may or may not be scraping into or away from the point of attack. If the tackle stunts to the outside on occasion, we simply tell the four-back to look for him, and we send the *guard* to the onside linebacker. In essence, the setback looks to the outside for the stunt, the guard to the inside.

Although the blocking scheme may not be as devastating, hence as much fun, against the split 6 as against the 5-2, it has proven to be very effective for us, primarily based upon the relative predictability of the split 6. More important, the alignment gives us *at least* as many men at the point of attack as has the defense.

The 4-4 defensive alignment, particularly the stack on our offensive guards and ends, presents a totally different situation because of the absolute unpredictability of the stunts. Our use of the Pro 3 and Pro 4 alignments, therefore, will capitalize on one of the acknowledged weaknesses of the 4-4 stack defense. In essence, we will resurrect one of our principles mentioned earlier—we'll "trap 'em."

THE SETBACK TRAP

We'll trap them with the setback in order to provide the fewest possible keys *if* the linebackers are keying through the guards. The best play sequenced off the "Pro 4/Quick at 4" action is illustrated in figure 6-4.

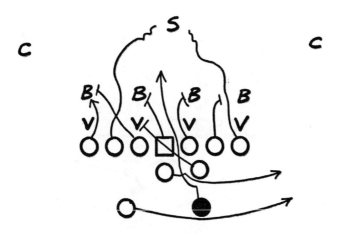

Figure 6-4 "Pro 4/Quick slant setback trap at 1"

In the huddle, the play will be designated "Pro 4/Quick slant *setback* trap at 1."

We haven't seen the defensive tackle yet who can react very effectively to that blocking scheme, particularly the first few times we call it. The last thing a defensive tackle expects early in the game is to be trapped by a back out of the backfield. By releasing the offensive left guard to the outside of the tackler, we, in effect, set him up to be trapped.

Relative to execution, all the quarterback does is open directly toward the four hole. The right halfback takes one step toward the four hole and then pushes off his right leg in order to make a diagonal entry into the one hole behind the fullback's block. Because the quarterback is operating down the line of scrimmage, the play involves an outside hand-off to the running back, who is effectively shielded from the defense.

This is not to say that we don't like the Pro 4/Quick at 4 versus the 4-4 stack. It, too, is an excellent play. Consider figure 6-5. First of all, we capitalize on the double-team block on the defensive tackle. As with the noseman on a 5-2, we don't care *which* way he decides to stunt. If he does stunt into the center/guard gap, we simply have the right tackle plateau to the offside backer or to one of the safeties. He can't adjust his path quickly enough to pick up the stacked onside backer. The setback has *that* assignment anyway.

The outside stack is handled by an inside-release from the offensive right end. If the down-man in the stack comes to the inside, the end simply shield blocks him. If the up-man comes to the inside, the end can block him more aggressively. Obviously, the running back is instructed to stay close to the blocks on the inside stack because they are more predictable.

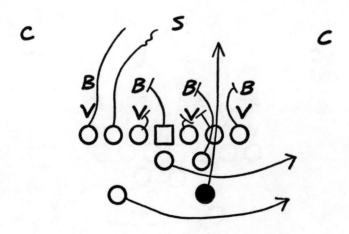

Figure 6-5 "Pro 4/Quick at 4"

Once we establish even a moderate threat with the "Pro 4/Quick at 4," we're ready to run the "Pro 4/Quick slant setback trap at 1." Obviously, as the game wears on, such play-action can become a little tedious for our setback because most offensive backs aren't used to blocking defensive tackles. So we try to use it only as a sequenced alternative to our basic play action. We also, however, have put our third guard on that position—or our third tackle, depending on what we have in mind for that particular game.

Consider figure 6-6, a "Pro 4/Power right." It illustrates another dimension of the 3 and 4 setback alignments. Once the defensive tackle starts slanting back to the inside or is realigned to compensate for the overload at the four hole, the power play at six or eight is a good variation on the "north and south" attack. We use regular power blocking with a two-team on the tackle. If the tackle is slanting away, the end is instructed to plateau to the onside linebacker. The setback "hammer blocks" the outside man on the line of scrimmage, and the right halfback leads the ball carrier through the hole or around the end, depending on the direction of the setback's block.

Having run the power play a few times with success, we are ready to run the "Pro 4/Power counter at 5," as illustrated in figure 6-7. As with all our counter plays, we like to use the tackle trap because it gets at least one of the tackles out of the trenches for awhile and it *doesn't* provide much of a key to linebackers who are reading through the guards for trap action.

The play is illustrated against a 5-2, but it is equally successful against

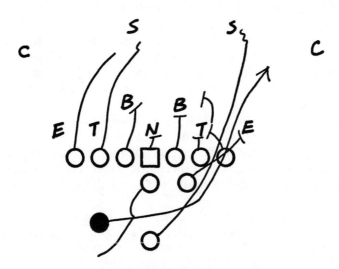

Figure 6-6

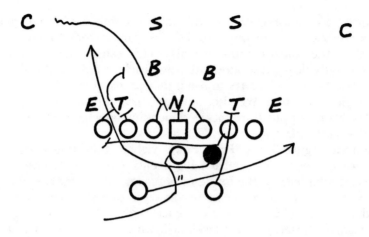

Figure 6-7

a six-man front or any of the 4-4 alignments. A couple points to remember involve, first of all, the need for the offensive line to tighten
down their line splits in order to prevent interior penetration. Second,
the offensive left end is instructed to double-team the defensive tackle—
unless he's stunting away from the point of attack, in which case the end
is told to plateau to the onside linebacker.

Third, the center and the two guards are told to triple-team the noseman, assuming of course that the linebackers are not blitzing. Depending
on the noseman's stunt, one of the guards will not have to block him.
That guard is instructed to head downfield to block the onside safety.
His block usually is the touchdown block.

Finally, the setback is told to pivot and take a position step parallel to
the line of scrimmage, hesitating just long enough to give the pulling
tackle time to clear. He then times his speed until he receives an inside
hand off from the quarterback, who drops straight back after completing
the exchange.

The play is one of the quickest-hitting counter plays you will ever see
and serves as an excellent complement to our basic plays, particularly
once the defense begins to gang up at our four hole to compensate for
the offensive overload. If they decide to do that with a safety on a
cornerback as illustrated in figure 6-8, we'll throw the "Pro 4/Power
counter at 5 action pass" at them.

A recent state championship game involved just this defensive adjustment. It was well conceived. If the play was at four, the cornerback
was in a position to fill quickly. If it was off-tackle or around the end,
he could get to the outside quickly to help out.

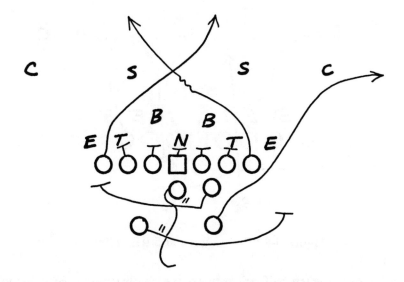

Figure 6-8

But if it involved our counter-action, it immobilized the corner just long enough for us to pick on the middle safety, who suddenly found himself being briefly stalked by two receivers and then unable to cover either of them. They were both open for a big gainer.

THE PLAY-ACTION COMPONENT

We will describe more of our passing attack later. Obviously, most of the passes involve play-action due to the restrictions of the four-set formations. It is also important at this point to recognize that we can run the power setback slant trap at 1 or 3 or use any combination of additional plays using the 4-set. Certainly, you will create a variety of your own, influenced in large part by the dictates of your own offensive philosophy.

We will mention a final play because it has been surprisingly successful for us. We call it simply "Pro 4/Quick at 3/RH influence." Figure 6-9 illustrates the play against a split 6. We like it particularly well when the defense becomes conscious of the four hole and starts to compensate by either placing an extra man on that side of their defensive alignment or stunting into that area of our offensive alignment.

All we do is send the setback down on the safety, influence at the four hole with the right halfback, and reverse-open the quarterback before

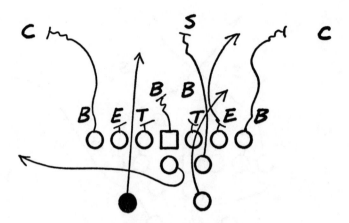

Figure 6-9 "Pro 4/Quick at 3/RH influence"

he hands to the left halfback at three. We simply straight-block the hole and rely on the defense to adjust or stunt themselves out of position.

If the sequence provides nothing else, it shows the defense that a Pro 4 formation does not necessarily mean a quick at four. It means that we can also throw the "Pro 4/Rev op Quick at 3 action pass," as illustrated in figure 6-10. It is a special pattern and, as evidenced in the pass routes, is the perfect complement to the blocking action on the Quick at 3. The key receivers are the setback and the right end, who both put heat on

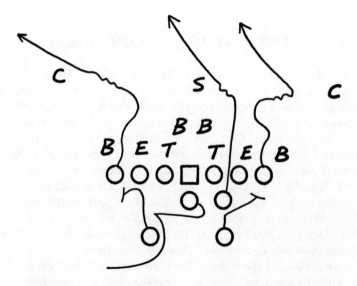

Figure 6-10 "Pro 4/Rev op Quick at 3 action pass"

the safety by stalking their respective defenders and then breaking deep in the middle zone. This play was a game breaker for us recently against one of our toughest opponents.

Obviously, we can do much more from the Pro 4. So can you, depending on your style of play. We also can bootleg from power action; we can sweep, and we can run the veer to both sides. We can speed option, and we can run a variety of counters. But the fundamental point has been made. The Pro 4 formation provides a powerful overload at or near the point of attack that gives an attack defense all it can handle.

LET'S WRAP IT UP

The overload at or near the point of attack accomplishes a few important strategic advantages. First, it provides another blocker at the point of attack. Second, the defense's adjustment to the overload usually forces them out of one of their favorite alignments and provokes them into an alignment that is generally foreign to them. Third, the adjustment is usually their *only* adjustment, so they end up in an alignment that is more predictable for the offense.

Finally, against a defense that frequently sends its linebackers, the Pro 4 positions a blocker equally close to the point of attack to intercept him. That may be the formation's biggest advantage, particularly when the setback in the hole is used with other backfield alignments—the focus of the next chapter.

7

The Wing 4 and the I 4: More Variations

If you still retain a doubt or two about the effectiveness of the three- or four-set concept, perhaps this chapter will provide the answers to your questions. First of all, the I 4 and the Wing 4 are fundamentally the same as the Pro 4 set. The strategic advantage of having an effective runner/blocker in the 4-set position is consistent, regardless of the backfield alignment.

If your questions refer to the more substantive issue of its workability as an offensive formation, we have but one more recommendation. Try it. Apply to the formation some of your imaginative best in terms of what you are accustomed to doing offensively. Make some slight modifications, and we're sure that you'll discover, as we have, that the formation is as good against attack defenses as anything you can throw at them.

As evidenced in the previous chapter, it certainly doesn't provide for a wide open brand of football or give the fans the razzle-dazzle type plays that bring them to their feet. All it does is win. We much prefer to bring our fans to their feet when we're kicking off to our opponent.

It loads up the offense at the point of attack and takes away one of the clear advantages attack defenses try to retain throughout the game, namely the ability to confuse the blocking schemes of the offense. The 4-set formations take away that advantage by providing an offensive overload and by creating double-team blocks *somewhere* near the point of attack.

In essence, we try to create a situation where the defense's gaming has no effect on what we plan to do offensively. If we are unable to *predict* what the defense plans to do, then we opt for the next best situation. We establish blocking schemes and overloads that make prediction unnecessary. With linemen who have mastered the double-team/plateau block, the offense has developed its own unique "strike force," one that is capable of using the defense's stunts to its own advantage.

Having provided another sell job for the 4-set formation, let's look at the Wing 4 and the I 4 in terms of the new wrinkles they provide. Obviously, the Pro 4 precludes the possibility of any inside belly and outside belly option action. It does not rule out veer option, quick option, or speed option possibilities, but it does take away our inside belly action and all of our cross fire action.

Whenever our football team is blessed with a particularly talented fullback, we want to use him as much as we can. In some games, therefore, we will line up in the Wing 4 and/or the I 4 formation in order to keep the fullback in his home position.

These formations provide a symbiotic relationship between our program and our fullbacks. We have had fullbacks who went on to play for Notre Dame, Princeton, and Iowa, because they were excellent athletes. They also came out of an excellent program, one that provided the strategic framework within which they could display the full range of their talents.

GOOD PLAYERS AND GOOD PLAYS

Barry Switzer, the legend at Oklahoma, once told us that good players make good plays. No one can deny his grasp of the obvious. But we believe that the reverse is just as obvious: good plays make good players. College coaches are likely to agree with Coach Switzer because they *recruit* blue chippers. High school coaches are likely to agree with him *and* with us, because they *make* blue chippers.

And they make them with plays such as the one illustrated in figure 7-1, "the Wing 4/Cross fire at 2 lead." The play is diagrammed versus the 5-2 *and* the 6-1. Against the 5-2, the cross fire lead at 2 is fundamentally the same as our other "lead" plays described earlier. The center and onside guard are instructed to double team the noseman, unless he's slanting away from our point of attack. If he slants away the guard will plateau to the offside backer.

Once again, the tackle inside-releases to the safety. If the defensive tackle is coming hard, the offensive tackle may have to stay with him. Normally, however, if he can escape to the inside, the defensive tackle will never get to the fullback, who has been instructed to favor the double-team block on the noseman. If the setback does his job blocking the onside linebacker, the play is a gainer. It can't help but pick up yardage, particularly if the defense plays a routine slanting or scraping-type stunt action.

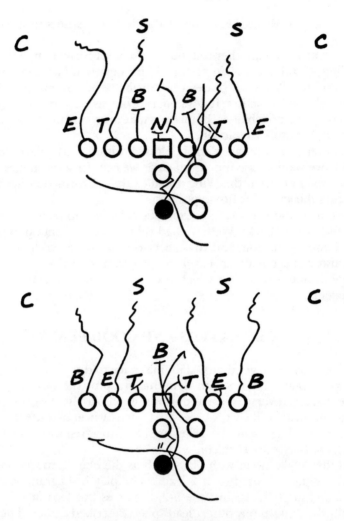

Figure 7-1 "Wing 4/XF2 lead"

Obviously, and as mentioned previously, if the onside backer is executing a scrape with the noseman and stunts himself *away* from the point of attack, the center and guard will block the noseman, and the setback will look to the inside for the offside backer's adjustment to play action. If there is no adjustment, the setback will continue directly toward the safety.

The obvious difference between the Wing 4/Cross fire at 2 lead and the Pro 4/Quick at 4 lead or, for that matter, the Full House/Cross fire at 4 lead is simply the backfield action. In the case of the Wing 4/Cross

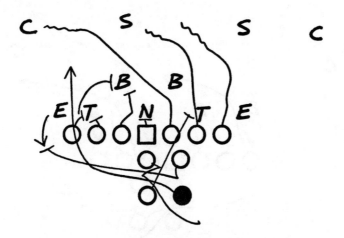

Figure 7-2 "Wing 4/XF setback trap at 5"

fire at 2, we're running the fullback into the two hole and faking the right halfback away from the point of attack.

Obviously, the backfield action gives us an excellent complement to the Cross fire at 2 lead. As illustrated in figure 7-2, the "Wing 4/Cross fire setback trap at 5" can cause problems for *any* attack defense. Running the Cross fire action from the Wing 4 formation gives us two distinct advantages, particularly when used in conjunction with the series provided by the other 4-set alignments.

One, by having the setback trap the defensive end on the five-man front, we don't provide any obvious keys to the inside backers. Any good backer will watch his backfield key *through* the appropriate offensive linemen. Our guards, in any 4-set formation, provide no keys. The second advantage is that the Cross fire setback trap at 5 accommodates very nicely the defense that tries to take our fullback away from us by jamming the defensive tackles down the line of scrimmage, particularly *away* from the strongside of the offensive formation.

An offensive left tackle can take the defensive tackle all by himself, and our left end, no longer needed to double-team their defensive tackle, can go immediately to the onside linebacker, who already is being preoccupied by our left guard *and* the fullback's fake at two. It's a good play, and we get a lot of mileage out of it.

PROTECTING WITH THE SETBACK

The third play in the sequence, diagrammed in figure 7-3, is the "Wing 4/Cross fire bootleg pass at 8." This particular play will use the setback as the personal protector on the right side. The advantage of using the

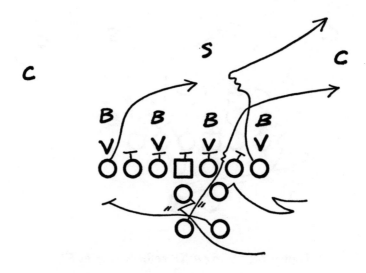

Figure 7-3 "Wing 4/XF bootleg pass at 8"

setback instead of one of the guards as the personal protector against a
pure attack defense is that it enables us to keep our guards at home to
prevent any earlier defensive penetration.

As is evidenced in the illustration, the play is fundamentally the same
as any bootleg action out of the full house or out of any of our other
several backfield sets. The fullback, while making his fake at the two
hole, is to look for a safety blitz. In the absence of such a stunt, he
continues through the guard and tackle gap, hesitates a count, and sneaks
into the flat in front of the cornerback. Keeping the guards at home
against the 5-2 defense provides us relative assurance that we can get
our fullback open somewhere underneath the cornerback, particularly
if the fullback realizes the importance of getting lost in the line before
sneaking into the secondary.

The fullback generally is the widest open of the three receivers. But
if the backs execute good fakes and the right end sells his stalk on the
safety, he is sometimes wide open to the outside behind the cornerback,
particularly if the secondary is covering "over and under" to the outside.
We also have hit the *offside* end on the play, when we get one who has
the moxie to find the open area behind or between the linebackers.

As with all bootleg plays, the quarterback must execute his backfield
fakes very deliberately, hesitate after faking to the halfback, even watching him for a split second as if the halfback has the ball, and then release
hard to the outside to set up behind the setback or to take whatever the
defense gives him to the outside. Depending on down and distance and

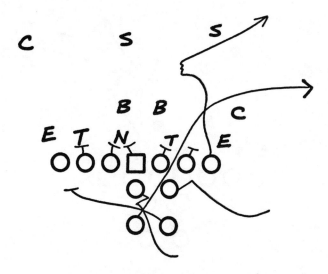

Figure 7-4

the skills of our quarterback, we also give him the option of running the ball.

Obviously, the play is very effective against a defense that tries to make some kind of a strongside adjustment to our Wing 4 formation. A recent state championship game resulted in the adjustment in figure 7-4. Notice its inability to handle the bootleg pass.

Against the 5-2 defense, particularly if the defense stunts routinely with slant or scraping action, the Wing 4 formation also provides a bootleg flood to the outside. Figure 7-5 illustrates the "Wing 4/Cross fire bootleg flood pass at 8. In this particular play, we're using the onside guard as the personal protector because the fullback is filling for him.

Obviously, if the onside linebacker is coming or if the offside linebacker is scraping into our two hole, the fullback will have to block him. He will *not*, however, have to *sustain* the block. All the fullback has to do is force the linebacker to the *inside* and then release on his pass route. Certainly the quarterback will be able to deliver the ball before a blitzing linebacker can adjust his path and get to him.

If neither of the linebackers stunts, the play is a sure thing, *if* the backfield executes its fakes, and if the fullback runs a smart pattern, looking for the open area in the defense while he is hesitating momentarily on the line before releasing. Remember also that the play, even if unsuccessful, gets the defense's attention and causes the secondary to hesitate the next time the end or setback releases on a stalk/shield block on run action.

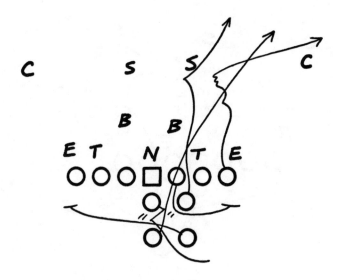

Figure 7-5

THE BOOTLEG SCREEN

Now, let's take the whole sequence just one step further, as in figure 7-6. We call it a "Wing 4/Cross fire bootleg at 8 action/screen left." How many times have you seen the backside rush versus a bootleg completely disregard the faking halfback, particularly if he appears to be taking the play off? Normally, when the defense determines bootleg action, they compensate as fast as they can to backfield action. The linemen, therefore, don't even have to roll to the outside to set up the screen. All they need to do is allow the pass rush to "beat them" to the inside, then take two or three steps to the outside in order to set up in front of the right halfback.

As you can see in all these plays, the backfield action is fundamentally the same, but the areas we attack in the defense are significantly different. That's the beauty of our offense against attack defenses. They can never really be sure just where we will hit. Their game plan, therefore, must accommodate a wide range of possibilities. *No* defense enjoys such a prospect.

One more word about the screen pass. We are very careful not to allow our lineman to simply open the door and then turn around and gawk while the quarterback runs for his life. They are expected to execute a solid two-count block and then release to their screen positions as fast as they can. Once they reach those areas, they are to set up in a hit position. The center is to look to the inside for any fast-reacting

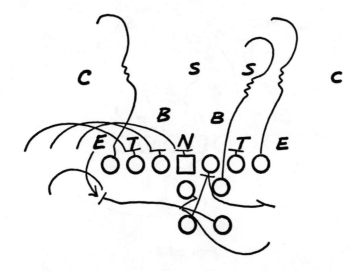

Figure 7-6 "Wing 4/XF bootleg at 8/Screen left"

linebackers, and the tackle and guard are to be prepared to block the first defenders to challenge them.

This play, as with many of our screen plays, has been very effective for us, particularly against teams with a strong backside pass rush. It is especially effective when run from bootleg action. Obviously, the bootleg action can be run from a variety of backfield sets. We can *power* bootleg from the Pro 4, but we probably have had the greatest success with the play out of the full house formation. That particular play will be discussed and illustrated in a subsequent chapter.

For now, let's get back to the Wing 4 and to one of our bread and butter plays, as illustrated in figure 7-7, the "Wing 4/Quick at 4." Like the "Wing 4/Cross fire at 2," the Quick at 4 goes right at the defense, pits our best against their best, and seeks simply to overpower the opponent at the point of attack. Obviously, we try to catch the defense in an alignment that is unable to handle the additional blocker at the point of attack.

As evidenced in figures 7-8 and 7-9, the "Wing 4/Quick at 4" is effective against both an odd-man and an even-man defensive front. Figure 7-7 illustrates the play versus a 5-2, the defense using one or any combination of the stunts and "games" that are available to them. Figure 7-8 shows the play versus the split 6 and the stacked 4-4, two very popular attack alignments.

Because the split 6 tends to be somewhat more predictable than the stacked 4-4, we get a lot of mileage out of the Quick at 4 versus that particular defense. We even do quite well with it versus the 4-4 because

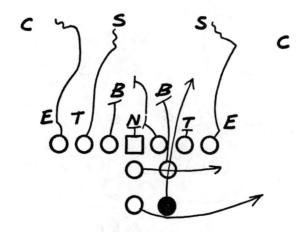

Figure 7-7

of the need to block only one of the two men in the outside stack. All our right end has to do is step through to the inside and pick up whichever of the two slants to the inside.

The play still gives us a double-team block versus the 5-2 and the 4-4, and it gives us welcome angles versus the split 6. Versus the 4-4, for example, we don't care *which* way the inside stack is stunting. We have them effectively eliminated from the play no matter what they do. Much the same is true versus the 5-2.

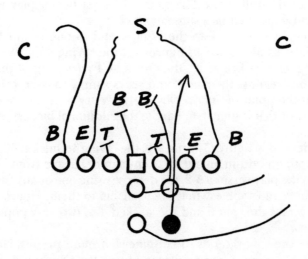

Figure 7-8

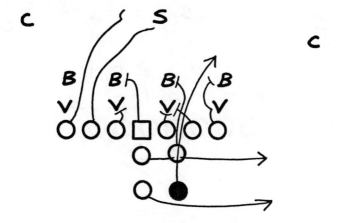

Figure 7-9 "Wing 4/Quick at 4"

THE RIGHT SEQUENCE

The split 6 may give us just a bit of trouble, particularly if their onside defensive tackle is a good football player. So we like to set up in the same formation and, as illustrated in figure 7-10, run the "Wing 4/Quick at 6" at them. Obviously the right halfback's fake is critical if the play is to be effective. If he *does* run an effective fake, one that takes him on a collision path with the onside linebacker, he can help jam up the inside to give the fullback more running room at the six hole. The timing of

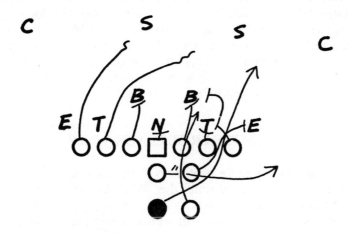

Figure 7-10 "Wing 4/Quick at 6"

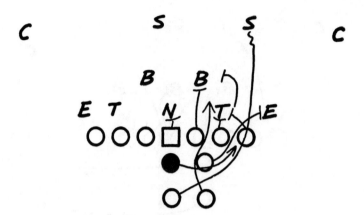

Figure 7-11 "Wing 4/Quick QB keep at 6 or 8"

the play also is critical if the hand off to the fullback is to be effectively shielded by the halfback's fake.

We fell short one year in our bid for another state championship, but the loss certainly wasn't the fault of the play diagrammed in figure 7-11, the "Wing 4/Quick Quarterback keep at 8." We had been having good success with the Quick at 4, nothing much beyond 4 yards, but it was enabling us to pound away at what was one of the best defenses we had seen all year.

So once they became conscious of the halfback at four, we showed the same backfield action, only we had the quarterback keep the ball at eight. All he did was flash fake to the halfback, hesitate momentarily while the fullback cleared, and then follow him to daylight. As evidenced in the illustration, the four-back is responsible for the outside man on the line of scrimmage; the fullback is instructed to read his block and to lead the quarterback to the open area. The combination of the Quick at 4 and the Quick quarterback keep at eight marched us right down the field for a quick third quarter score. Then the god of fumbles reared his ugly head . . . but we won't get into that.

ANOTHER SETBACK TRAP

Let's look at just one more play from the quick series with the Wing 4 alignment. Figure 7-12 illustrates the "Wing 4/Quick slant setback trap at 1." We don't use it often, but it's always effective, particularly against the even-man front, when we instruct the lineman at the point of attack to *outside*-release on the defensive lineman to be trapped. The outside-release makes the setback's trap easier, and it gives us the option of trapping the linebacker if he is blitzing into the guard/center gap.

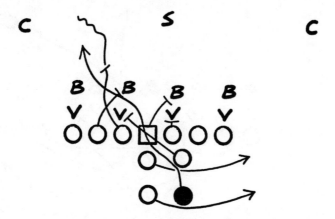

Figure 7-12 "Wing 4/Quick slant set trap at 1"

Because the quarterback's body is between the line of scrimmage and the ball carrier, we get a shielded hand off—and one of the best and quickest misdirection plays in our offense. It also provides for great play-action when we want to throw the ball, but that will be the focus of a future chapter.

THE POWER TOSS

A final play from the Wing 4 formation is one of football's oldest, but it takes advantage of the natural strength of the formation. We call it a "Wing 4/Power toss right." Figure 7-13 illustrates the strategy. Rather

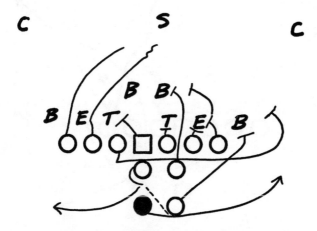

Figure 7-13 "Wing 4/Power toss right"

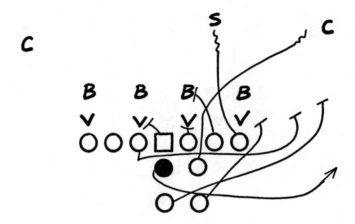

Figure 7-14

than race all our blockers and the ball carrier to the sidelines in an attempt to beat the defensive pursuit out of bounds, we try to eliminate the pursuit before it gets started.

Rather than have the setback lead the play around the right end, we send him right at the linebacker. The right tackle and right end two-team the defensive tackle, or the ends plateau to the linebacker or safety, depending on the slant of the defensive tackle. It's a power play, nothing less, nothing more—and it has been good to us, particularly when you consider the relatively weak containment potential of certain attack defense alignments.

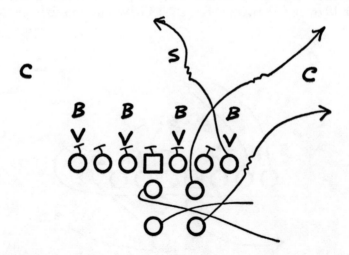

Figure 7-15 "Wing 4/Right rollout/Right Alabama Flood"

Consider figure 7-14 as a further example. The play is a "Wing 4/Right roll out run at eight." It's diagrammed versus a stack 4-4 to illustrate further the formation's potential for eliminating pursuit before it gets started. Not only does it cut down an immediate pursuit, it also provides a natural play-action passing complement, one that is easily sequenced.

Figure 7-15 illustrates the "Wing 4/Right rollout/right Alabama flood." The rollout action gets our quarterback away from quick defensive penetration, and it puts a lot of pressure on what is already relatively weak defensive containment. The cornerback and the safety in particular are in a real bind, especially if the pass "*de*ceivers" do a good job selling run.

Just a moment of creative thinking reveals that there are all kinds of running and passing plays that can be run from the Wing 4 formation. We don't have to spread players the entire width of the field, for example, to pose an effective passing threat. All we have to do is be sure to provide well-conceived passing complements to our running action—and we can do just that from our Wing 4 formation.

THE I 4

We also can do it from the I 4. Unlike the Wing 4, which is predisposed to the obvious strength of the formation, the I 4 provides a more balanced backfield set, one that can attack the weakside just as quickly as it can the strongside of the formation. We like it particularly against a team that makes a quick defensive adjustment to the obvious offensive overload at the four hole.

Before they make such an adjustment, however, and assuming they will remain in their favorite defensive alignment, we'll capitalize on the original advantage of the four-set and overload at the point of attack with a play such as the "I 4/Power at 2 FB lead," as illustrated in figure 7-16. The play is illustrated versus a 5-2 and a 4-4 and probably is one of our most consistently effective plays. It is a power play in its purest sense and virtually eliminates the confusion of defensive stunts. Frankly, we don't care *where* the defense goes because of the double-team and angle blocks created by the offensive formation.

The same is true of the "I 4/Power at 6," as illustrated in figure 7-17. This particular play is designed to beat the defensive end who keys the movements of the offensive end. Most defensive ends/outside backers who key the offensive end will take one or two steps with him when he outside-releases.

Even just one step opens the six hole for us, particularly with the setback on top of him before he can react back to play action. With the fullback leading through to pick up any seepage, we have found the play to be very effective. Obviously an outside scrape or a safety blitz hurts it. We can't be perfect every time. On the other hand, however, the play

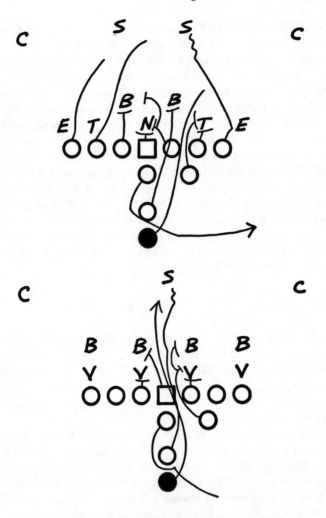

Figure 7-16 "I4/Power at 2/FB lead"

is a killer for a defense that jams its defensive tackle to the inside to take away the fullback up the middle.

TAKE WHAT YOU CAN GET

So—you take what the defense gives you. They all give you something, even the best and least predictable attack defense, and they give you more and more as *you* become less and less predictable.

We all know that any attack defense is going to gang up on the offense that won't or *can't* pass the football. Complementary play-action passes

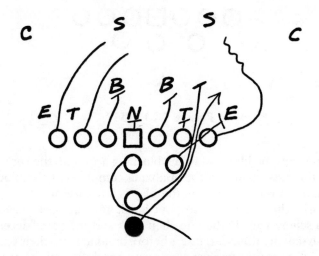

Figure 7-17 "I4/Power at 6"

are essential, unless the offense wants to try to grind out an occasional yard or two against a nine or even a *ten*-man defensive front.

That's why we like the "I 4/Power at 6 action/Right Alabama." Figure 7-18 illustrates the Alabama pattern. We can run others. They will be described in Chapter 10. For now, the point to emphasize is that the

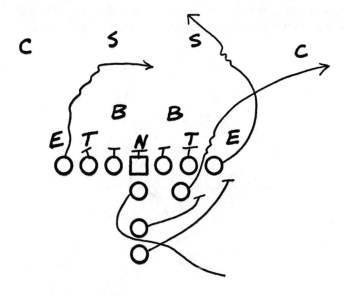

Figure 7-18 "I4/Power at 6 action/Right Alabama"

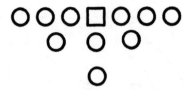

Figure 7-19 "I34"

pass routes must be identical to the blocking action on the running play. Because the pass routes in the Alabama complement the blocking responsibilities in the Power at 6, the play is a natural for us.

Obviously, the line has to fire-out block and the backs have to do a good job selling run. If they do their jobs and the pass "deceivers" do a good job stalking their defenders before breaking into their pass routes, the play will pick up some yardage, even break the game wide open.

THE I 34

Finally, let's take a look at the I 3-4 formation as illustrated in figure 7-19. The logical extension of everything we've discussed so far, the I 34 gives us an offensive overload on both sides of the center. Obviously, we can run the "I 34/Inside belly lead at 4" as illustrated in figure 7-20. We also can run with equal ease the inside belly at *three* lead.

More important, with motion, we can run almost everything we have discussed up to this point, and the balance of the initial formation doesn't

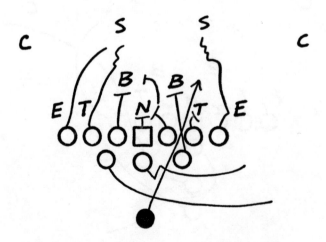

Figure 7-20 "I34/Inside belly at 4 lead"

give the defense a "strongside" adjustment. Motion is mentioned in Chapter 11, so we will save the I 34 formation for later.

LET'S WRAP IT UP

The strategic effectiveness of the four-set formation from almost any backfield set has been established in terms of the strength it provides at the point of attack and its potential for beating the attack defense out of its basic game plan. The kinds of plays that are executed are restricted only by the coach's imagination and by his offensive predispositions.

We have had great success with all the four-set formations. Obviously, their effectiveness is either enhanced or limited by the characteristics of our opponent's defensive alignment and game plan. We have had greatest success when we have surprised our opponents with the formation. But even when we don't surprise them, they have to plan for it—even if we don't decide to use it. The busier we can keep them with things we don't do, the more effective we'll be with things we *do* use.

We can resurrect the four-set formations at any time during the game or use it with motion as our primary game plan. Whenever we make the decision to use it, it is guaranteed to give the defense fits. That is why you should find a place for it in your offense.

8

Run to Daylight with the Deep Power

The emphasis so far has been to disregard the unpredictability of attack defenses by creating double team and angle blocks somewhere near the point of attack and by overpowering the defense at one point along the line of scrimmage. The strategies have been very effective for us and constitute the primary thrust of our running offense against attack defenses.

But we have another strategy, one that capitalizes on the kinesthetic spontaneity of a natural runner—when we find ourselves gifted with one. We call it the Deep Power and run it from the I formation. We have discovered that it is very effective when it comes to exploiting the need for most attack defenses to penetrate into the backfield.

We simply allow them to penetrate. The line pass-blocks on every deep power play, unless it involves a trap. On traps they are assigned specific down-blocking responsibilities. In essence, we allow the defense away from the point of attack to make their initial charges and then take them whatever way they want to go.

The tailback lead steps parallel to the line of scrimmage with his onside foot, takes two more steps, plants with his onside foot, and drives hard toward the line of scrimmage. While he's taking his three parallel steps at 1/2 to 3/4 speed, he is watching the line of scrimmage for daylight—anywhere along the line. Our primary point of attack is off-tackle or around end, depending on what the defense gives us. But we instruct our tailbacks, particularly the one(s) with great kinesthetic sense, to run to daylight. We have had tailbacks run right straight up the field for big gainers simply by reading the defensive stunts.

106

PRINCIPLE NUMBER ELEVEN: WAIT FOR
STUNTS TO COMMIT

Here's how we do it. First of all, all the interior linemen are instructed to pass block initially. The play call in figure 8-1 is "I 8/Deep Power right," and is illustrated versus the 4-4 stack because the 4-4 is one of the toughest for us to block effectively. Given our inability to predict which of the two players in the outside tandem will assume outside responsibility, we instruct the onside offensive end and tackle to pass block until one of the two commits, then double team him. The fullback will block the defender who shows to the outside.

After pass blocking for one full count, the offside guard pulls and leads the play to daylight. His one-count delay places him in a perfect position to lead the tailback, who has taken his three parallel steps before receiving the ball from the quarterback. Obviously, the strategy is easier versus an odd-man front, but, if covered, the guard simply invites the defensive lineman to an outside-release and then pulls to lead the tailback.

The quarterback reverse opens and sprints to a spot approximately two and a half yards behind the onside tackle. After making the exchange, he continues dropping hard to set up for pass, even showing the left hand as the tailback starts running with the football. His right hand should be hidden at his side, simulating a "hipped" ball.

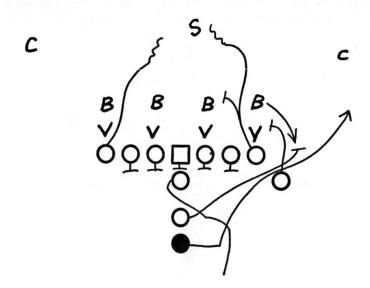

Figure 8-1 "I8/Deep Power Right"

Our purpose is to have the quarterback execute run and pass action exactly the same way. If he does his job well and if the line effectively shields the defensive line charge, even a moderately good back is going to find some daylight, and a good one may consistently pick up first-down yardage. The deep power for us has never broken the big play, but it often has resulted in a steady diet of four- and five-yard attempts. And that's enough to demoralize even the best attack defense.

THE WRONG READ

The defensive secondary has a tough time, too. All good pass defenders will try to read an offensive tackle in addition to their primary pass keys to determine if the offense is executing a run or a pass. The offensive tackle's pass block on a running play does a good job of immobilizing the secondary and of thoroughly confusing them when we play-action pass from the deep power series.

As with all teams, we like to reserve the "over" call when we run into an overshifted six or a 5-2 monster, as in figure 8-2. The play call in the huddle is still "I 8/Deep Power right." On the line, however, the quarterback will shout "over" so that the play becomes a deep power left.

The left tackle now invites the defensive tackle to the inside. If the defensive tackle accepts the invitation, the left end simply plateaus to the onside linebacker, who is likely to be reacting to the play, unless he's on a predetermined stunt to the inside. If so, the end releases immediately to stalk the safety. Oftentimes, the linebackers will drop to their

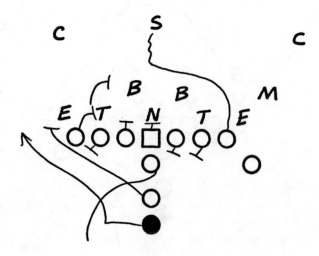

Figure 8-2

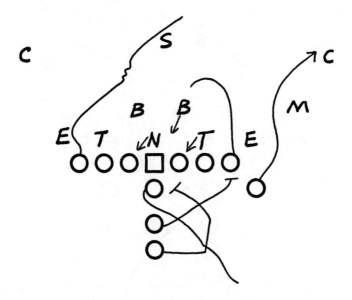

Figure 8-3

hook zones anyway once they see the guards and center set up to pass block. As a matter of fact, they will just about every time unless they're on a predetermined stunt.

If they are coming most of the time or a good percentage of the time, we will call the "I 8/Deep Power right action/strong hook," as diagrammed in figure 8-3. The "strong hook" always involves the strongside tight end; the "weak hook" always involves the weakside tight end. All the end does is set up in his pass block the way he normally would on the deep power play, watch the linebacker to see if he's coming, and then release immediately into the vacated hook zone. Obviously, the play is just as effective against an even-man front.

If we happen to guess wrong, and the linebacker *isn't* coming, we have the tight end run a complementary pattern with the wingback as illustrated in figure 8-4. The offside end always runs a deep angled pattern to clear the secondary—and is often open as a trailer when the linebackers aren't blitzing, as in the illustration. Obviously, this play capitalizes on an earlier principle: exploit the holes in the secondary.

Again, we emphasize the fact that a defense that attacks is giving up *something*. When they send linebackers, they are giving up the hook zones. Our job is to exploit that weakness. We do it by releasing the tight end into the area vacated or by calling the "I 8/Deep Power right/screen left," as evidenced in figure 8-5.

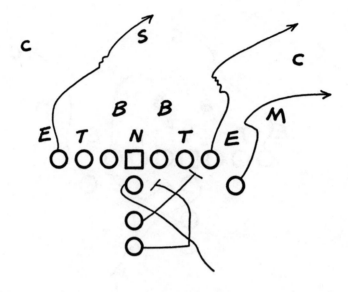

Figure 8-4

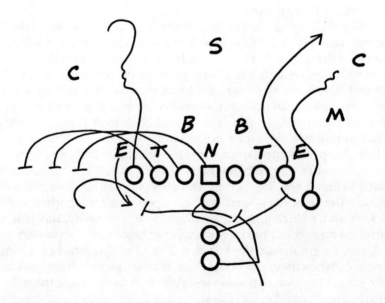

Figure 8-5

A LITTLE DECEPTION

The play is *very* deceptive. First, it attracts attention to the strongside run possibility. Then, it suggests deep power *pass* action. The tailback is effectively forgotten once he sets up to pass block. As with the bootleg screen mentioned earlier, too much has been happening for the defense to process. By the time they determine pass action and recover to their zones, the screen play has been executed.

The blocking schemes for the line remain consistent with everything else we do from deep power action, with a couple of exceptions. One exception involves the play diagrammed in figure 8-6, the "I 8/Fullback quick at 21 trap." Whenever this particular play is run from the I formation, the quarterback sells deep power action after handing the ball to the fullback.

The play is illustrated against a 5-2 because that is the defense we run into most often. I suspect that a *really* innovative coach could have the line set up in pass pro and invite the defenders away from the point of attack, but we haven't experienced that kind of illumination yet. So we have remained with the blocking scheme diagrammed in figure 8-6. Besides, we want the play to hit quickly, so we've stayed with a more traditional blocking scheme.

Much the same is true of the "I 8/Deep Power counter at 5," as illustrated in figure 8-7. With this particular play, our only deviation from

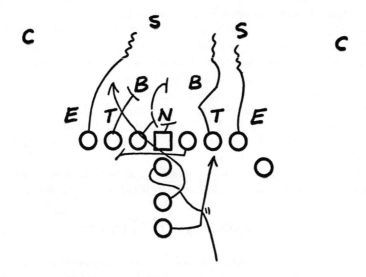

Figure 8-6 "I8/Fullback Quick at 21 trap"

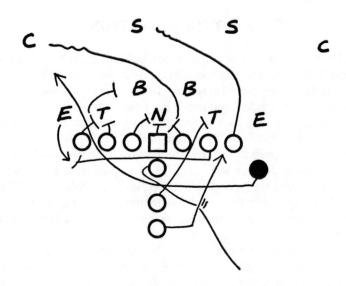

Figure 8-7 "I8/Deep Power counter at 5"

tradition is the tackle trap. We like the tackle trap with all our counters. It doesn't give the linebackers any clues, and it gives the tackles a chance to do something other than bang heads in the trenches.

They like it. So do we—when we watch the game films and see one of our biggest and best *cascading* down the line of scrimmage and literally running right over a defensive end/outside backer.

The initial *triple*-team block on the noseman also helps to bring the linebackers up a step or two, who are expecting to fill at the point of attack. Obviously, the guards are told to watch for them when initiating their blocks in case the linebackers are coming.

The play is a good one because it absolutely nullifies the effect of a tough, stunting noseman. It also accommodates almost anything the linebackers can do and it gives us a solid double-team block on the defensive tackle with the option to plateau to the linebacker or the safety. It also satisfies one of the principles suggested by the coaches at the University of Wisconsin, namely, to use misdirection against attack defenses. We'll discuss that particular principle later in the book.

THE PASSING COMPLEMENT

For now, let's look at another principle to be discussed later—one suggested by Notre Dame—the use of play-action passing. Deep power action is about the best we can use against any tough defensive charge.

Chapter 10 deals with the subject of play-action passing in considerable detail, so let's just whet our appetites with one example of the strategic effectiveness of deep power action.

Figure 8-8 illustrates the "I 8/Deep Power right/Right Delaware." Keep in mind that the offensive line has been pass blocking on most deep power running action, so the secondary is already a dollar short when it comes to reading pass. The key to the play's success, therefore, is contingent on two things: one, how well the backs execute their fakes and, two, how well the pass "deceivers" stalk the defenders before breaking into their pass routes.

Remember that we already have instructed the quarterback to extend his arm and show his left hand after giving the ball to the tailback. Then he is to proceed hard on his dropback move and set up in his passing position. Obviously, he does the same thing when the ball is being passed.

To increase the faking on the play, we teach a specific technique. After the quarterback receives the ball from the center, he reverse opens, holding the ball in both hands and beginning to extend it toward the tailback, who is still taking his initial three steps parallel to the line of scrimmage. Once the tailback plants his foot and pushes toward the line of scrimmage, he starts to make his pocket to receive the ball.

The quarterback approaches, puts the ball in the tailback's pocket, then removes it, placing it vertically on his hip. He leaves his hand in the tailback's pocket and allows it to trail as the tailback approaches the

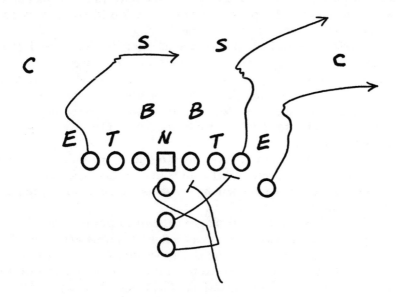

Figure 8-8 "I8/Deep Power right/Right Delaware"

line of scrimmage. He then continues his drop, plants his back foot, and snaps into his passing position.

The rest of the faking is up to the fullback and the tailback. To sustain the complementary relationship between the running and passing action from the deep power series, the fullback is instructed to block hard to the outside, almost as hard as he does on a running play.

The tailback is told to take his three steps parallel to the line, plant his foot and then drive hard toward the line of scrimmage, giving every appearance of running the ball. As he makes his fake, he is watching the line for any kind of penetration—a blitzing linebacker or an unblocked defensive lineman. The tailback's responsibility is to pick up any interior penetration; the fullback is to block to the outside.

If the backs do their jobs convincingly and the ends and wingback do a good job stalking the pass defenders before running their pass routes, the play is a gainer. Sure, those are big "ifs," particularly in high school football. That's why our job goes well beyond "strategizing."

MORE THAN BLOCKING AND TACKLING

Let's admit it. One big concern at the beginning of the year is to get everybody in the right places and then try to identify those "favored few" to play key positions on offense and defense. "Blocking and tackling" has been the name of the game ever since Jim Thorpe donned his sheet metal shoulder pads; and games, like World War I skirmishes, have been won or lost "in the trenches."

But modern football has almost as much room for finesse and deception as for blocking and tackling. So we find in our program the need to emphasize faking from day one. It may be less a factor against attack defenses than against read defenses, but it still does a mighty fine job deceiving the secondary and, often, the linebackers. You know as well as we do that one good fake is sometimes more effective than two or three good blocks.

So when the deep power series is introduced, we watch the timing and the faking very carefully. Without both, the play, whether it's a pass or a run, won't cause the momentary hesitation in the secondary required to make it successful.

We have several additional plays in the deep power series, but the argument has been made. It just makes sense to give a solid, kinesthetic runner enough time to read the defensive stunts and then to run to daylight. The kid who has learned to trust his body when he runs with the ball can always find a little daylight, and he can drive attack defenses crazy.

THE OUTSIDE BELLY

An excellent complement to the deep power series and the inside belly series from the I formation, the outside belly series can give fits to containment personnel, particularly against four- and six-man fronts. Figure 8-9 illustrates an "I 8/Outside belly at 6" versus the 6-1, the split 6, the 4-4, and the 5-2. It involves the onside guard and provides angles on all the defensive personnel.

The wingback is instructed to release two to three yards straight ahead, angle to the inside, and stalk either the onside linebacker or the safety, whomever shows first. The only exception involves a defense with an outside stack. Against the stack 4-4, for example, the wingback is told to take a lead step toward the stack and to block the man who goes to the inside. The other blocks remain fundamentally the same.

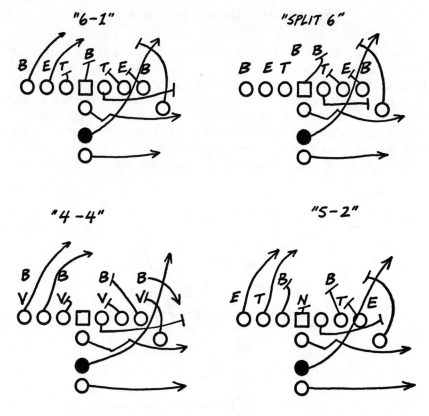

Figure 8-9 "6-1" "Split 6" "4-4" "5-2"

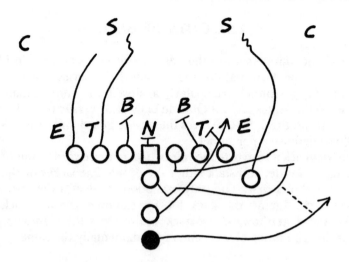

Figure 8-10 "I8/Outside belly option 8"

Obviously, the outside belly is an option series, designed to put the outside man on the defensive line in a no-win situation. A well-drilled team probably could option the fullback at the six hole, then give or keep contingent on the defensive end/outside backer's reaction to the fullback. We normally don't run the play that way. The potential for fumbles is too great. So the play normally is predetermined: outside belly at 6 or outside belly option at 8, as diagrammed in figure 8-10.

Notice that the onside guard always leads the play around the end,

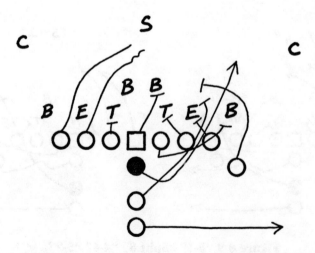

Figure 8-11 "I8/Outside belly at 6 follow"

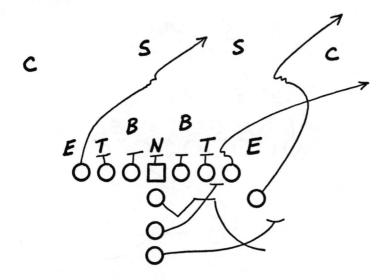

Figure 8-12 "I8/Outside belly/Right Delaware"

looking back to the inside to guarantee that the quarterback and tailback have only the cornerback to contend with. When the play involves the fullback at 6, the pulling guard turns upfield and kicks out the cornerback. He *never* blocks the outside man on the defensive line.

The only time the defensive end/outside backer is blocked is when we call the "I 8/Outside belly at 6 follow," as illustrated in figure 8-11. In this case, we make just a perfunctory fake to the fullback to keep the outside man dropped off, then the fullback blocks him and the quarterback follows through the six hole. This is yet another of our "lead" and/or "follow" plays in which we use one of our backs as a blocker.

This play is surprisingly effective, probably because of its complementary relationship to the rest of the series. It also serves as an effective backfield sequence for our play-action passing attack. Figure 8-12 illustrates the "I 8/Outside belly right/right Delaware." The pass pattern is a Delaware again because that particular pattern complements the blocking responsibilities of the pass receivers.

We can call other patterns as well, one of which has been particularly successful for us. It is simply a one-man pattern, designated in the huddle "I 8/Outside belly right/left end deep slant." Figure 8-13 illustrates why it has been so effective. The wingback and right end are doing exactly what they do on the running play and are likely to influence the defensive safety and cornerback.

All that is required is that the blocks of the end and wingback immobilize the two pass defenders in order to allow our left end to get behind them on his deep slant. Obviously, the play isn't worth much on

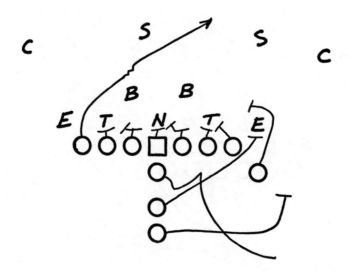

Figure 8-13 "I8/Outside belly right/Left end deep slant"

third and long, but on a second and four, it's a real killer. Any one-man pattern is effective if called at the right time and executed well by the key players involved.

LET'S WRAP IT UP

This is true of everything we do. But we can help matters if the plays we design capitalize on *our* strengths and *their* weaknesses. So far, much of what we've discussed does just that. The more angles we can create on blocking schemes, the closer our passing plays resemble running plays, the easier it is to create a blocking overload at the point of attack— the more pronounced and perplexing the problems of the defense, even the attack defense.

Certainly we run a lot more from the I formation: cross fire action, inside bellies, speed option, and a variety of power plays, all with very effective counter plays and play-action passing complements. But so do you. We wanted simply to highlight *our* deep power play as another way to cloud the issue for attack defenses.

Now let's focus on a few ways to attack the middle. Very frankly, that is where we have had our greatest and most exciting successes.

9

Attacking the Middle

The Cross fire at 12 trap probably is our most successful play. We indicated earlier that our fullbacks have ended up at such notable football powerhouses as Iowa, Princeton, and Notre Dame. The 12 trap is one of the reasons. Obviously, each of the fullbacks was blessed with generous doses of talent, but the traps at 12 and 21 did a great deal to help showcase those talents.

Invariably, our fullback is our leading ground gainer. He seems to be the heart and soul of our offense. If he runs well, everything else seems to fall into place, and much of his running occurs within the cross fire series. As illustrated in figure 9-1, it involves crossing action in the backfield, and as such, provides an element of simple misdirection.

The play call in figure 9-1 is a "T 8/Cross fire at 1" and represents a quick opener for our fullback. The illustration involves straight blocking, although we can block it several different ways. The quarterback simply opens into the fullback, gives him the ball, hand fakes the left halfback, and continues hard to the outside on a bootleg fake. Several years ago, the "Cross fire at 1" was a big play for us.

Now it is a big play for the defense when we run it. Attack defenses like to play teams that straight block. *They* don't do *anything* straight. The result is confusion for the offensive blocking scheme. Imagine a simple scrape with the onside linebacker and noseman, as illustrated in figure 9-2. The noseman will jam the one hole, and the left guard will either be chasing the linebacker or, if he's smart, releasing immediately to the safety.

His block will make little difference, however, because the noseman already will have plugged the hole. The center has not been constructed who can snap the ball and seal off a jamming noseman. So we run the Cross fire at 1 only occasionally, but we complement it often with the "T 8/Cross fire at 12 trap," as diagrammed in figure 9-3. Now the stunting noseman makes no difference to us. The onside guard is instructed to

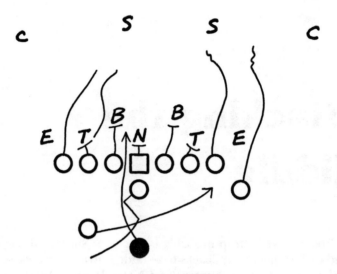

Figure 9-1 "T8/XF1"

double-team him. If the noseman stunts away, the guard simply plateaus to the offside linebacker. If the *onside* linebacker is scraping, as in figure 9-4, we simply two-team the noseman and let the linebacker go. Our tackle then is instructed to shield block the first man to come in his direction, usually the *offside* linebacker.

The "trap 'em" principle shared by Notre Dame makes sense again. We don't care what the linebackers do. The blocking scheme accom-

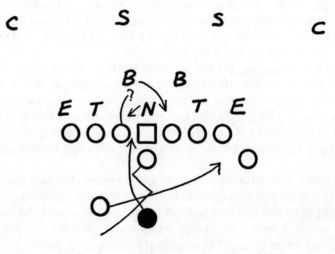

Figure 9-2

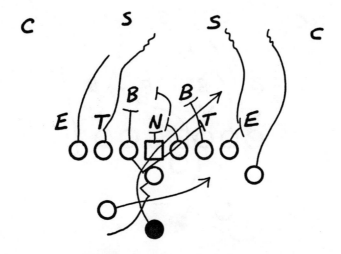

Figure 9-3 "T8/XF 12 trap"

modates almost any kind of inside stunt, and it works equally well against an even-man front.

Figure 9-5 illustrates the same play with the same kind of "trap/down blocking" versus the 4-4 stack. A defensive left tackle jamming the guard/center gap will cause the play some problems, but we will take that chance. The chances are equally good that the entire line will be slanting to their *left* as well, in which case the play is bigger than ever.

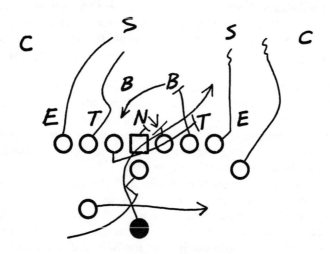

Figure 9-4 "T8/XF 12 T"

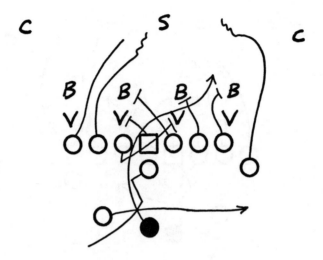

Figure 9-5 "T8/XF 12 T"

It even works well versus the split 6, as evidenced in figure 9-6. Again, the tackles jamming hard to the inside cause the play a problem or two, but the split 6 hasn't effectively stopped the play yet, and we don't expect that it will. As a matter of fact, we look forward to a split 6 because we have so much fun with it.

UNJAMMING THE TACKLES

A lot of 5-2 attack defenses jam the defensive tackles hard down the line of scrimmage to take the middle away from us. It is a fairly routine adjustment. Some will also vary their stunts by jamming the tackle and *outside* scraping with the linebacker to protect themselves in the off-tackle hole.

Obviously, the outside scrape doesn't hurt us when we are running the 1-2 trap or its mirror, the 2-1 trap. We've already admitted that the tackle hurts us somewhat—but not a lot in the 5-2, because the play already is starting to the left of the center. So, if for no other reason than to keep the defense guessing, we vary the cross fire attack and trap the play at six as illustrated in figure 9-7.

The tackle is no longer a problem, and the end can plateau to the onside linebacker, who may or may not be on an outside scrape. Again, we two-team the noseman, unless he is slanting away, in which case the onside guard plateaus to the offside linebacker. The combination of the two is very effective, particularly if we throw in the full house alignment and thicken the plot with the cross fire at four lead, as described in an earlier chapter.

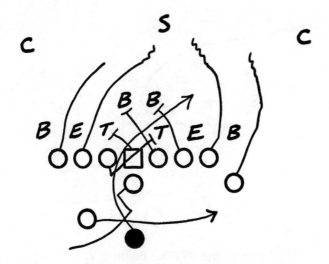

Figure 9-6 "T8/XF 12 T"

COUNTER THE ATTACK

Then, when we call the "T 8/Cross fire counter at 5," things get better and better. The play, as illustrated in figure 9-8, may not be our most consistent ground gainer, but as a complement to the rest of the cross fire action, it always provides the potential for a game breaker and a whole lot of entertainment for the fans.

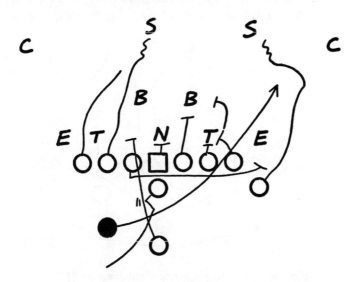

Figure 9-7 "T8/XF trap at 6"

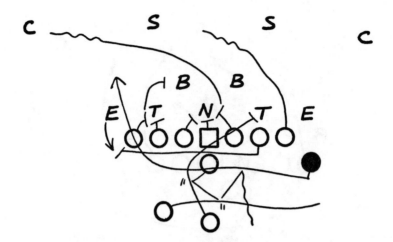

Figure 9-8 "T8/XF counter at 5"

Initially, the play involves a *triple*-team block on the noseman, *if* the backers aren't coming. It also involves a double-team block on the defensive right tackle. One of the two guards, depending on which way the noseman is stunting, will release to make the touchdown block on the cornerback. The onside safety is usually fading to his left or dropping to deep middle, based on the initial move of the offensive left halfback. The offensive left end again will either double-team the defensive tackle or plateau to the onside linebacker.

Again, we use the tackle trap on all counter plays because it provides no keys to the linebackers and gives us an overpowering trap block on

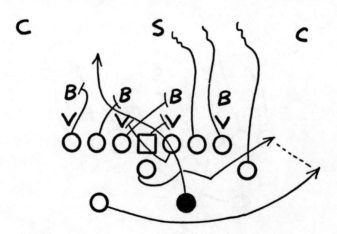

Figure 9-9 "Pro 8/Quick slant trap at 21"

the outside. The backfield action is 1-2 trap with the fullback filling for the pulling tackle. After completing the fakes to the fullback and the left halfback, the quarterback completes his pivot and hands the ball to the wingback, who is following the pulling tackle down the line of scrimmage.

Throw a cross fire counter action pass into the game plan, and the defense can be a day late and a dollar short throughout the entire game. We have even run the cross fire at 12 trap *with counter action* to confuse the defense even further. The linebackers and secondary picking up the wingback often forget all about the fullback, who is running right in front of them. Our line even yells "counter!" when we do it—to help matters along.

THINKING QUICK

How many times have you found yourself in a real battle, the kind in which neither team seems able to sustain anything? We all like to be in the situation in which we feel at least one or more plays ahead of our opponent, in which we always feel sure of what we are going to do next. We can control such games.

But how about the guessing games, the ones in which we keep searching for something to sequence, something to sustain? We usually can count on our Cross fire at 12 trap for some yardage, so we can stick with fundamentally the same blocking scheme and go with the *Quick* at 21 trap out of the pro set. The play, as illustrated in figure 9-9, gives us the same play as the Cross fire at 21 trap but with a different look.

It also gives us an excellent option sequence versus the 4-4 stack and most other attack alignments. When we run the option, which is diagrammed in figure 9-10, we still reverse-open the quarterback and have him flash-fake the ball to the dive back, who fills for the onside guard. The onside guard leads the play around the end when the play is designated "Pro 8/Quick slant option at 8" in the huddle.

When the play is designated "Pro 8/Quick slant Quarterback trap at 6," as in figure 9-11, the pulling guard traps the outside man on the defensive line. Again, the right end takes whichever of the two in the outside tandem goes to the inside. The wingback still goes right to the safety to cut off his inside-out pursuit path. Normally, the cornerback takes himself out of the play when he sees the option develop to his side.

Again, the key is sequencing and being able to build on a predictably successful play. The 1-2 and 2-1 traps have provided just that for us over the years. They have gained a lot of yardage for us and have given us the opportunity to run several other plays that complement them.

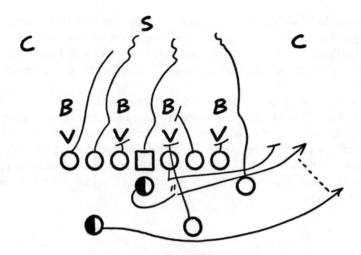

Figure 9-10 "Pro 8/Quick slant option at 8"

LET'S WRAP IT UP

This has been a quick chapter—no pun intended—but it has discussed one of our most consistently successful plays against *any* kind of defense. Our best plays over the years, as a matter of fact, have been the kind we can run against any defensive alignment *or* predisposition. Attack defenses make no difference to us when we gear up our squad for a

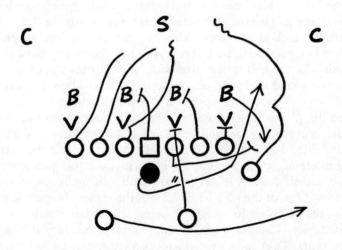

Figure 9-11 "Pro 8/Quick slant QB trap at 6"

game. They provide a few new wrinkles, but the principles we have enumerated thus far do more than compensate for them.

The cross fire series and the quick series have provided the staple for our offensive attack because they can be run from a variety of backfield sets and because they provide a solid foundation for our play-action passing attack—which is the focus of the next chapter.

10

The Passing
Component

PRINCIPLE NUMBER 12: KEEP THE ATTACK DEFENSE OFF-BALANCE WITH THE PLAY-ACTION PASS

Attack defenses swear up and down that they have their tails covered when it comes to stopping the run *and* the pass. But what defensive team, no matter how gifted with hard-nosed personnel, can commit seven or eight players to jam the gaps on the line of scrimmage—and still cover all the zones in the secondary?

They do a lot of talking, but our experience has proven that a quarterback with even a moderately quick release can pick them apart. We'll show you how—after we provide a quick explanation of our system.

THE BIG PICTURE

As soon as a pass play is called in the huddle, the quarterback should have a mental picture of the eventual locations of all his receivers. He should envision variable penetration into the secondary and have at least a general idea of the yardage to be covered within each pass route—before and after cuts are made. He should know which receivers will be delaying or *delayed* at the line of scrimmage, and he should "see" which of them will be cutting first on crossing action.

These mental images are critical—absolutely essential to the eventual success of a good play-action passing attack. They don't take into consideration other essential bits of knowledge, such as the differential speed of receivers, their mobility, and their relative pass-receiving skills. Hopefully, the good quarterback will master those considerations as well.

We also hope that he will keep down and distance in mind in order to predict his receiver's depth of penetration into the secondary and to predict with *some* certainty the kind of coverage the secondary is likely to deploy. Maybe he'll even know his receivers well enough to establish that level of unspoken communication that results in a broken pattern and a game-breaking completion.

But the mental image of where his receivers will be is still the single most critical element in establishing a sound play-action passing attack. The quarterback who doesn't have such a mental picture either decides on a single receiver before the ball is snapped or races through his backfield fakes perfunctorily in order to get his drop to find out where everybody is.

Even then, he usually finds only one or two of them, and they are well covered because he did nothing with his backfield fakes to immobilize the secondary. A backfield that fails to acknowledge the value of faking might as well use a conventional passing attack all the time. Play-action is a waste of time.

So we work on faking as much as we work on pass routes; and we work long and hard on pass routes. Pass routes for the conventional dropback passing attack are fundamentally different from the routes in a play action passing attack.

PASS DECEIVERS

The ends and backs in a conventional passing attack are appropriately pass *receivers*. In a play-action passing attack, they are pass *deceivers*. Their initial job is to convince the linebackers and secondary that they are executing a running play, that their stalking maneuvers are preliminary to a block, not to a pass pattern.

These delay tactics not only influence the secondary but they provide the time the backfield needs to complete all their fakes. The quarterback needs to hide the ball before he sets up to pass. If the pass receivers race through their pass routes, the way they might in a conventional drop back attack, they won't sell *run,* and they'll condition the quarterback to make sloppy fakes in his haste to set up and pass the ball before his receivers get out of range.

So, when we describe our primary eight patterns, we'll diagram them two ways: one in a drop back attack, the other from play-action. We have patterns other than these. We have three or four different three-man flood patterns, and we throw such standards as the quickie and the timed-quick out to the flanker or the split end.

But most of our passing involves one of just eight plays so that the quarterback can picture each one while he's calling it in the huddle. When we call a "T 8/Inside belly at eight action/Right Alabama," we want the quarterback to know exactly where his receivers will be when he completes his ride to the fullback and takes his two to three option steps before he drops back to pass.

A "create your own combination" concept just doesn't get the job done because by the time the quarterback receives the ball from the center, he's probably forgotten at least two of the primary three receivers. We want him to know where all *three* of them are. So we restrict our otherwise feverish imaginations to just eight plays.

We designate our plays in such a way that even the dullest light on the field can learn them all in a matter of days. Take the first play, the Alabama. Illustrated in figure 10-1, this play call is "T 8/Dropback/Right Alabama." The formation tells each player what pattern to run.

The Alabama requires the widest man on the side of the play call to run a banana in, the second man in on the side of the play call to run a slant out, and the widest man to the other side of the play call to run a post. Regardless of the formation, the assignments remain consistent.

If we wanted to run a pattern back to the weakside of the formation, therefore, we might call "T 8/Fullback power left action/*Left* Alabama." Figure 10-2 illustrates the same assignments to the weakside of the for-mation. The left end—the widest man on the side of the play call—runs the banana in. The left halfback—the second man in on the side of the play call—runs the slant out, in this instance, after bumping the defensive end. And the widest man *away* from the play call—the wingback—runs the post.

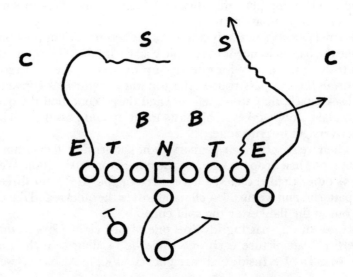

Figure 10-1 "T8/Dropback/Right Alabama"

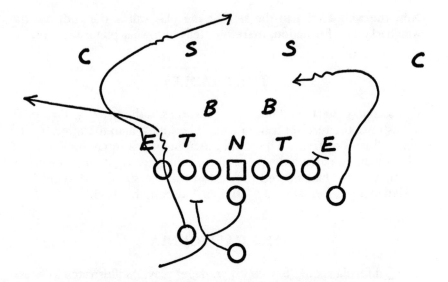

Figure 10-2 "T8/FB Power left/Left Alabama"

Each of our patterns is organized the same way. The assignments start with the widest man to the *side of the play call* (not the strong side of the formation), and ends with the widest player away from the side of the play call. So if we wanted to isolate a tall end on a short safety, we might call a "T 6/flex/Dropback/Right Alabama," as illustrated in figure 10-3.

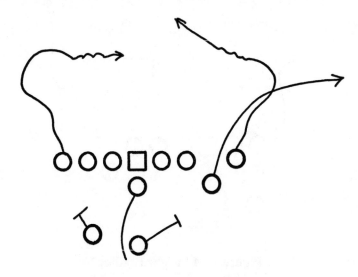

Figure 10-3 "Right Alabama"

Now the widest man to the side of the play call is the end, not the wingback. The formation, therefore, tells him what pattern to run.

THE BRADLEY

Our second pattern, and one of our favorites, is the Bradley. Figure 10-4 illustrates the receiver assignments. The widest man to the side of the play call runs a streak. The second man in runs a square out, and the widest man away from the play call runs the post. Again, the formation is a T 8. If we had wanted the end to run the streak, we might have designated the formation a "T 6 Split," as in figure 10-5.

THE CALIFORNIA

The California is our "first-down yardage" play. As illustrated in figure 10-6, every receiver runs a hook to the side of the play. If a *right* California, the receivers hook to the right; if a *left* California, they hook to the left. Obviously, they don't hook until they have gone two yards *beyond* what they need for a first down. We expect all our receivers to come back to the ball, especially on a hook pattern, so they need a two-yard cushion to execute the pattern successfully.

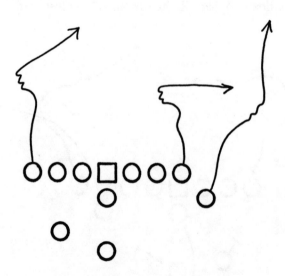

Figure 10-4 "Right Bradley"

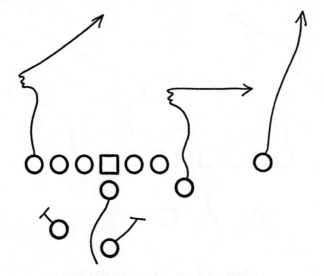

Figure 10-5 "Right Bradley"

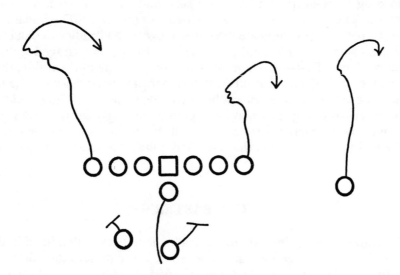

Figure 10-6 "Right California"

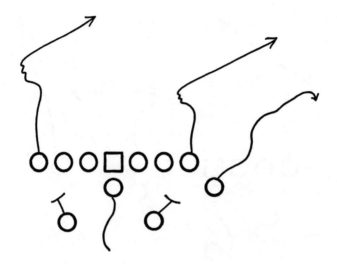

Figure 10-7 "Pro 8/Right Delaware"

THE DELAWARE

As illustrated in figure 10-7, the Delaware puts the safety, even in a rotating three-deep coverage, in a real bind. A *four*-deep has trouble with it. The key to the play is the wingback's out move. The initial part of the pattern must simulate the streak move in the Bradley so that even if the coverage is under-and-over, the cornerback is encouraged to think deep. The end's flag move must first jam the safety to the inside, then break on a diagonal. Obviously, the sooner the quarterback throws the ball, the better his chances will be to complete the pass. The secondary coverage—with *any* pass play—becomes increasingly *less* important the sooner the quarterback throws the ball. If the ball is in the air just as the end makes his break, the actual coverage is relatively unimportant.

THE EASTERN

We learned a long time ago that a double-in pattern with a flood in the outside zone *really* gets *our* attention, so we try to do it to the other guy before he does it to us. The play is especially effective against a very aggressive cornerback or a secondary that rotates fast on backfield action. Figure 10-8 illustrates the play run from a Pro 8 formation. But we have found that it is especially effective when we flank the right halfback and

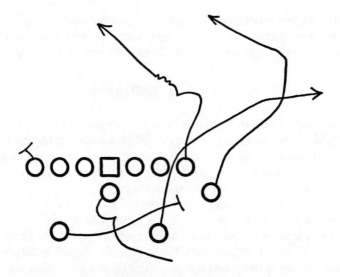

Figure 10-8 "Right Eastern"

call the "Pro *10*/Dropback/Right Eastern," as diagrammed in figure 10-9.

Running the play with a wide flanker generally provokes man-to-man coverage from the cornerback and ends up putting the strong safety in a bind. The play has been very effective for us, even when executed

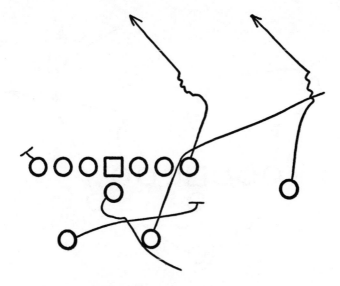

Figure 10-9 "Right Eastern"

somewhat differently from play-action. After we've described and illustrated each of our patterns, we'll summarize this section with a comparison of the differences between drop back and play action.

THE FLORIDA

Referring once again to Principle Number Seven, Entering the Secondary with Variable Speed and Penetration, let's consider the execution of the Florida pattern. As we discussed already in an earlier chapter, the Florida is particularly effective against teams that employ under-and-over or some kind of combination coverage.

Assume that the secondary has assigned to the cornerback the first out move or the first deep move in his zone. The safety has to pick up the first in move or help out on the second out move. As illustrated in figure 10-10, the "T 8/Dropback/Right Florida" drives *both* the cornerback and the safety deep and opens up the underneath area for the end. The wingback's 12- to 15-yard post influences both the cornerback and safety, and the end's 8- to 10-yard flag breaks somewhere underneath the coverage and to the outside. Even if the secondary is playing under-and-over, the end still has the potential to be open deep.

We have had considerable success with this play, in spite of the fact that secondary coverages have become so sophisticated. You and I both know that a crossing pattern, particularly one that varies speed and depth of penetration, can cause pass defenders a lot of trouble.

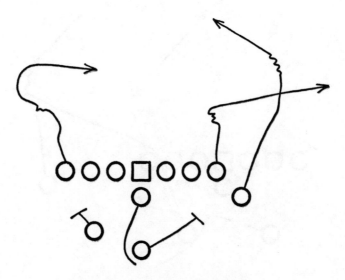

Figure 10-10 "Right Florida"

THE GEORGIA

Illustrated in figure 10-11, the Georgia is particularly effective when run from play-action. Again, the differences will be highlighted when we summarize this section of the chapter. For now, we'll consider only the pass routes when run from conventional drop back action.

The offside or free safety is likely to be keying the left halfback. The halfback's two to three steps to the outside should hold the free safety just long enough for the left end to slant hard on a diagonal across the field and flood the zone of the strong safety. Obviously, the play requires solid pass blocking at the line of scrimmage if we are to flood the strong safety's zone effectively. The quarterback, however, has the option to hit the left end immediately if his key, the strong safety, takes the right end right now on his deep inside move.

More will be said of this play when we discuss all the patterns in relation to the run action we've discussed in earlier chapters. Any time we flood the zone of one of the safeties, the other is going to have to help out. If play action prevents him from doing so, the secondary is in trouble. Perhaps that is why the Florida and the Georgia patterns have been so successful for us.

We learned some time ago that the best people to pick on with play action are the safeties and inside backers. They wouldn't be playing these positions if they didn't like to run into their fellow man. More important,

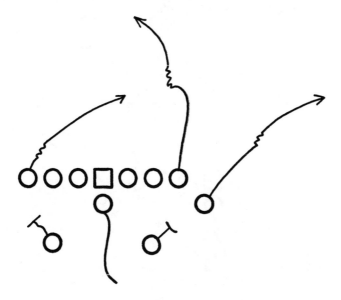

Figure 10-11 "Right Georgia"

their keys are players directly involved in run action. If those players sell run effectively, particularly on early-down plays, the safeties and backers can spend a good part of the day out of position.

THE HAWAII

The Hawaii, as illustrated in figure 10-12, capitalizes on the same principle. The wingback—or flanker, depending on where we decide to put him—starts out on a streak move. Then at approximately ten yards, he plants hard and drives back to the inside. The right end already has driven the strong safety deep and has broken to his flag move to challenge the cornerback.

The quarterback's key again is the strong safety. Even if he has released the right end on his outside move, he still is likely to be out of position, especially if the quarterback hits the wingback immediately after he makes his cut to the inside. The only person he has to be especially conscious of is the outside backer who may be dropping to the flat.

A FEW VARIATIONS

Those are the eight plays that constitute the primary focus of our passing attack. They can be varied by simply adding one word to each play designation. For example, we can vary the Alabama pattern simply by adding the word "change" to the play call.

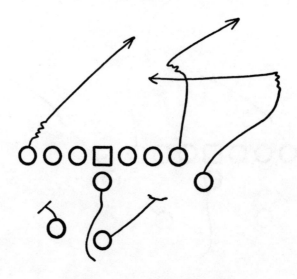

Figure 10-12 "Right Hawaii"

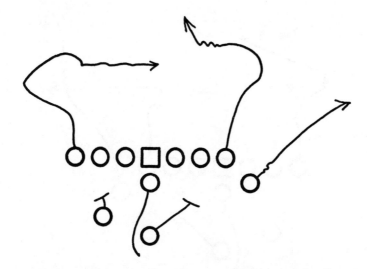

Figure 10-13 "T8/Dropback/Right Alabama Change"

Assume that we want to hit the wingback on a quick slant out pattern for first-down yardage. Figure 10-13 illustrates the play call, a "T 8/Dropback/Right Alabama *Change*." The wingback and the right end simply exchange responsibilities. Without the "change" call, the Alabama instructs the widest man to the side of the play call to run a banana in, and tells the second man in to run a slant out. The "change" call simply exchanges the patterns. We use the "change" call for all eight patterns.

We also add calls such as the "inside," the "stop," and the "comeback" to modify each pattern. The added word applies *only* to the outside receiver to the side of the play call. With the "T 8/Dropback/Right Bradley Comeback," for example, the wingback is the player affected, and he runs a pattern similar to the one diagrammed in figure 10-14.

If the added word is "inside," the wide man to the playside runs the pattern illustrated in figure 10-15, which is designated "T 6 Flex/Dropback/Right Bradley Inside." Remember, the player instructed by the additional word is always the widest man to the side of the play call; in this instance—based on the changed formation—it's the right end.

The final variation involves the word "stop." Again using the Bradley pattern as an example, the play call would be "Pro 8/Dropback/Right Bradley Stop" and would resemble the pattern illustrated in figure 10-16. The "stop" variation instructs the outside receiver to drive the defenders deep, then plant his outside foot and drive hard back to the ball. The timing is critical, but the variation is very effective against the secondary that uses over-and-under coverage.

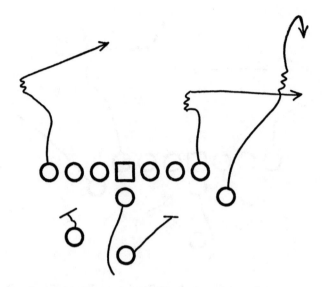

Figure 10-14 "Right Bradley Comeback"

Obviously, the three variations are called most commonly with the Alabama and Bradley plays, because the outside man's assigned pattern is suitable for such variations. We also use the stop and comeback variations with the Georgia patterns, but we designate "change" first, so that the wingback is assigned the deep inside route.

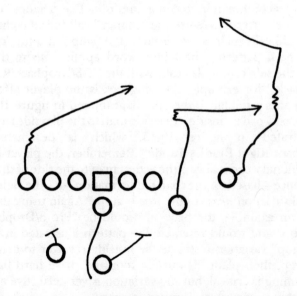

Figure 10-15 "T6 flex/Dropback/Right Bradley Inside"

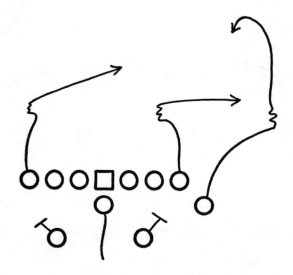

Figure 10-16 "Pro 8/Dropback/Right Bradley Stop"

Figure 10-17 provides a chart that identifies each play and explains the responsibilities of the receivers. Remember, we are not talking strongside or weakside. We're talking *formation* and the side of the *play call*. All plays, therefore, can be run to either side of the formation and can be varied with the "change," "stop," "inside," and "comeback" designations. Play with the idea for awhile. You'll see that the concept gives us significant flexibility but capitalizes on an easily remembered foundation of just eight basic patterns.

Here's the summary:

Name of Play	Widest Man to Play Side	Second Man in to Play Side	Widest Man Away from Play Side
Alabama	banana in	slant out	post
Bradley	streak	square out	post
California	hook out	hook out	hook in
Delaware	hook out	flag	post
Eastern	deep banana in	deep banana in	block
Florida	15-yard post	8–10-yard flag	hook in and slide
Georgia	flag	deep post	deep slant in
Hawaii	square in	flag	deep slant in

Figure 10-17

As you noticed, the Eastern is the only pass play that deviates from our basic rule of assigning responsibilities. The widest man away from

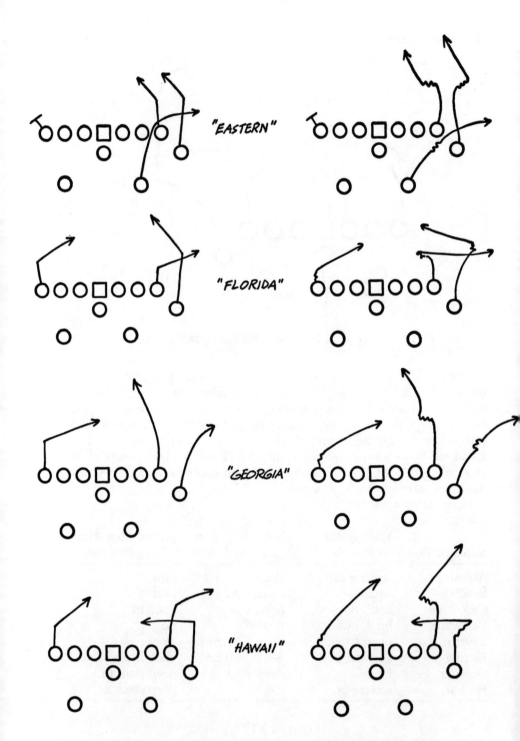

Figure 10-18 "Eastern" "Florida" "Georgia" "Hawaii"

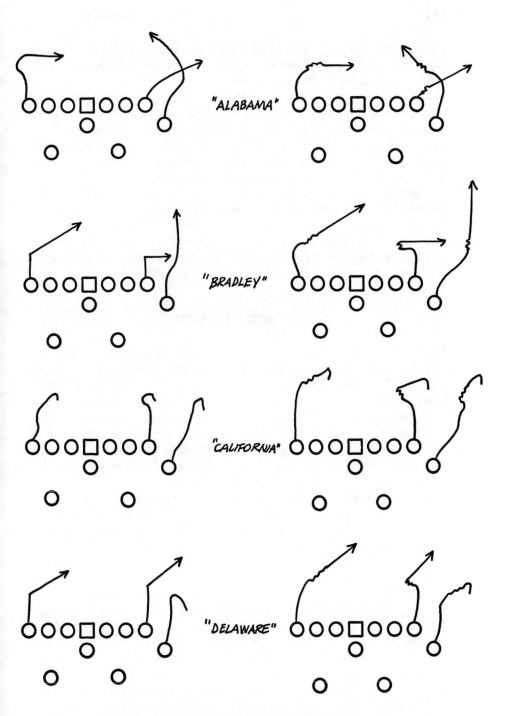

"Alabama" "Bradley" "California" "Delaware"

the play call, unless flanked or split, stays in to block. In the Eastern the third man in runs a moderate to deep flag in the outside zone after releasing from his backfield position.

Finally, let's provide a few quick illustrations of the difference between conventional pass routes and play-action pass routes. Figure 10-18 illustrates all eight pass plays. The left-hand box diagrams the play from drop back action; the right-hand box from play action. The squiggly lines in the right-hand boxes represent stalking a preliminary blocking technique prior to the final execution of the pass route.

The remainder of this chapter, with a few exceptions, will emphasize the pass routes as diagrammed in the right-hand boxes. "Play action" is the key to keeping the attack defense off balance. With that thought in mind, let's look at the formations and running plays we've discussed in the earlier chapters, combine them with the pass plays we've just described, and explain their effectiveness against attack defenses.

THE DOUBLE WING

We like the double wing for a lot of reasons. One certainly involves the fact that it forces our opponent to defend ten gaps along the line of scrimmage without providing an offensive tendency. With motion, it gives us virtually our entire offense. For our purposes in this chapter, it also gives us an effective passing threat on either side of the center.

Having forced a balanced defensive front, we can do a number of different things. Consider figure 10-19, a "Double wing/motion left/Inside belly at 5 action/Left Georgia." This is the pass play that is so effective for us from play action, and it is easy to see why.

The inside belly at three action, if effectively executed, will *at least* immobilize the onside safety. If the end's release and stalk move is convincingly done, the safety will be flat-footed for at least one count. That is all the play needs, considering the safety's zone is about to be flooded. Even if the offside safety drops to deep middle to help out, one of the two crossing receivers usually is open.

Consider the same backfield action—different pass play. Figure 10-20 illustrates the "Double Wing/motion left/Inside belly at 5 action/Left Alabama." Now the wingback—the cornerback's key—is stalking the safety, and the right end is blocking for at least one count. The right cornerback probably has "outside-in" responsibility on inside run action, so, given the fact that his keys appear to be blocking, he is likely either to take a few steps forward or to hesitate a moment or two to get a better read.

This pattern is particularly effective near the goal line, when the cornerback is forced to make an immediate decision. Our ends have scored a lot of touchdowns over the years with this play. They realize that if

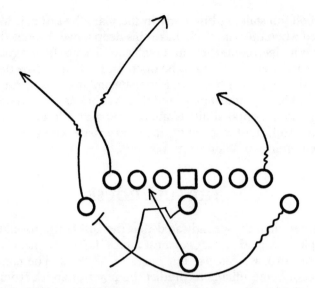

Figure 10-19 "Double wing/motion left/IB5 action/Left Georgia"

they want the six points, they had better execute a convincing one- or two-count block on the line of scrimmage before they release on the pattern.

At midfield, the safety is the player to pick on. He is likely to have an "inside-out" responsibility on any off-tackle action, so if the wingback

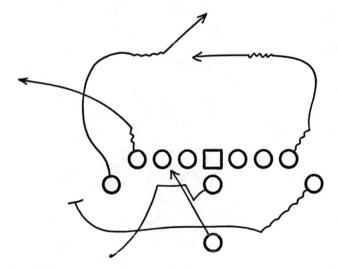

Figure 10-20 "Double wing/motion left/IB5 action/Left Alabama"

does a good job stalking him early in the play, the safety is likely to be flat-footed when the wingback makes his deep move. Even if the offside safety goes to deep centerfield and is able to pick up the wingback's deep move, the right end is going to be open on his slant across the field.

Obviously, we have a host of additional combinations of run and pass action. The eight standard plays and their variations give us considerable flexibility and the opportunity to attack almost any defense with just the right play. And, most important, the quarterback knows exactly where everyone is going to be on every play.

THE FULL HOUSE

In an earlier chapter, we indicated that the full house formation gives us a couple strong advantages against attack defenses: one, it reveals no strong side; two, we can use our backs as blockers. The combination, therefore, of being unable to predict the point of attack from scouting reports and of finding one hole overloaded with a blocking back puts the attack defense into the very dilemma that they're trying to create for the offense!

It also serves to create problems for them when we decide to play-action pass, particularly if they have a monster. We will not make that assumption, however; that would be making things a bit *too* easy for us. Instead, let's look at a full house formation versus a 5-2/4-deep defense,

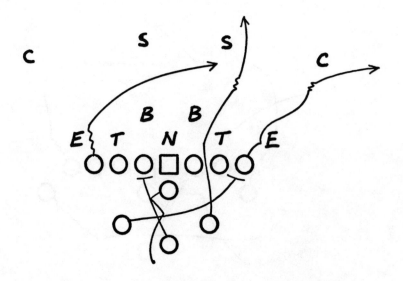

Figure 10-21 "Crossfire at 4 lead/Right Georgia"

as in figure 10-21. The play call is "Full house/Cross fire at 4 lead action/Right Georgia."

Notice how the pass play complements the blocking responsibilities on the running play. The right end blocks the outside man for one count, releases hard to the corner, stalks, and goes deep. The right halfback finds an opening in the line, stalks the onside safety, then blows past him. The offside end runs his deep slant after a moment's hesitation on the line of scrimmage.

This is why we like the Georgia pattern. It complements our run action from almost any set, and it gives us a flood in the zone of the safety who is most affected by the play-action. The only problem can be the offside safety who is dropping to deep centerfield. But he can't do a thing about the left end slanting deep across the middle.

The Bradley pattern also gives us excellent play action with the full house alignment. Figure 10-22 illustrates the "Full house/Inside belly option right action/Right Bradley." It has been a real game breaker for us, particularly against a cornerback who fills hard when he recognizes option action to his side. As important, the next time we run the option play, even if the pass *hasn't* been successful, the cornerback is going to remember the pass threat and fill somewhat more hesitantly.

Obviously, that also is a salient advantage of well-conceived play-action passes. The complement they provide the running game invariably strengthens not only the pass play but the run as well.

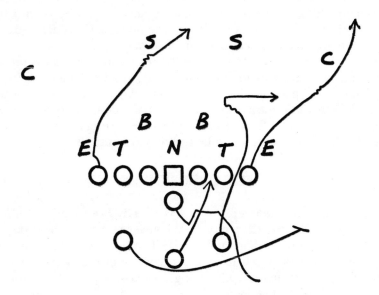

Figure 10-22 "IB option right action/Right Bradley"

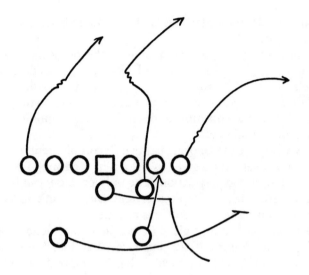

Figure 10-23 "Right Delaware"

THE 4-SET

Certainly, you have as much fun as we do creating combinations of passing and running plays for your play action attack. It's obviously important that you coordinate your own pass patterns with the 4-set alignment. But because you may want to borrow an idea or two from us, we'll throw one more example into the hopper. Consider figure 10-23, a "Pro 4/Quick at 4 action/Right Delaware."

Again, the complementary action between run and pass is obvious, and if the pass is thrown on first or second down, the element of surprise is enhanced. Surprise is a key factor in any play-action pass, but against attack defenses it's critical if we want to turn the tables on them. Surprise is *their* stock in trade. When we make it *ours*, we once again apply football's golden rule: We do unto them before they do unto us.

THE DEEP POWER

The argument for the deep power has already been made. Call it the sprint draw; call it the deep power. Whatever you call it, it works. The pass blocking with the line, and the deliberate backfield action makes the series a natural when it comes to confusing the defense with an unpredictable combination of running and passing plays, each run from fundamentally the same look.

A pass play that has been especially effective for us is the California.

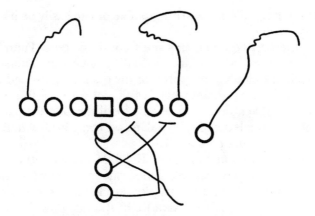

Figure 10-24 "Right California"

Figure 10-24 illustrates the "I 8/Deep Power Right/Right California." On third and three, third and four, even second and ten situations, the play has picked up critical first down yardage for us.

In a third and four situation, the defense, especially the linebackers and secondary, are concerned about filling *before* the ball carrier picks up the necessary first-down yardage. So—the shorter the distance needed for a key first down, the more anxious the linebackers and secondary are to help out at or near the line of scrimmage.

When we show pass blocking combined with a strong run capability, the linebackers and secondary don't know what to do. Then when we release the receivers to stalk the secondary as if preparing to shield block them, we gain an additional advantage. Normally what happens is the pass defenders go flat-footed and become victims of a well-timed outside hook pattern. The play is particularly good when all we need is three to five yards for a first down. The timing becomes more obvious as the distance for a first down is extended beyond that.

There are others. As a matter of fact, we can run all eight of our pass plays with all their variations from deep power action. So there is no need to provide more illustrations. All you have to do is mix and match—some of yours and some of ours.

THE WING T AND FLANKER SETS

Obviously, you can do the same thing from any Wing T formation. But before we conclude this chapter, we'd like to share a few more of our most successful play-action passes—run from a variety of Wing T formations. They use a variety of play action, some you may or may not have. If you don't, the plays are adaptable or can easily be incorporated within any system.

One of the best complements the Georgia pattern. Figure 10-25 illustrates the "T 8/Crossfire at 8 action/Right Georgia/Fullback release left." We admit that it's a mouthful for the quarterback—and more than enough to keep the defense's hands full. All we have to do is observe the right cornerback's reaction when we call the Georgia pattern. If he is influenced by the left end's deep slant, we come back with the fullback release. It's been a big play for us.

Another is diagrammed in figure 10-26. More than other play, it was a state championship for us. We added one more word to the play call to let the team know exactly what we were looking for and designated the play "T 8/Cross fire at 8 action/Right Bradley *Bomb*."

This is a play we time recurrently. It generally wraps up our passing drills. The quarterback makes quick flash fakes to both backs as he's dropping back. He then makes a five-step drop. The wingback stalks the cornerback quickly, then breaks deep as fast as he can run. Once the quarterback completes his drop, he turns and throws the ball as far as he can. We like to see a lot of air under it to give the wingback time to run underneath.

Obviously, the timing gets better and better as the season progresses. After a while the quarterback doesn't even have to see the wingback, just make his drop and air out the ball tight to the sidelines. The play was so consistently effective for us a few years back that the newspapers

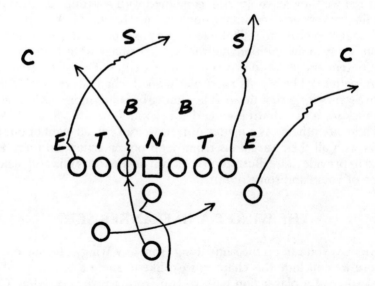

Figure 10-25 "Right Georgia/FB release left"

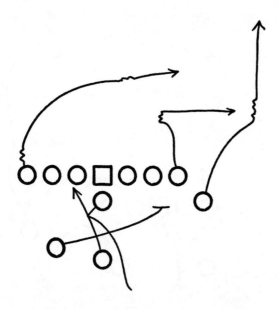

Figure 10-26 "Right Bradley Bomb"

started referring to our wingback as "Deep 6." The play got him a lot of free publicity, and it earned us a state championship.

We could go on and on about our play-action passing attack, but we have already shared sufficiently the nuts and bolts of what we do. You are invited to incorporate all or part of it into your offensive attack. The play and, more important, the concepts have been valuable contributors to our success over the years. Very candidly, we just cannot conceive of any football team handling attack defenses successfully week after week without a well-conceived and well-coordinated play-action passing attack. Ours has worked, and it will work for you.

LET'S WRAP IT UP

Before we conclude this chapter, it's important to acknowledge the fact that the conventional drop back attack can't be ignored. It doesn't make a lot of sense to stick with play action every time we run into a third and long situation, although we *do* like the deep power action. It comes as close to drop back action as anything else, and it retains the constant running threat that immobilizes the secondary and backs off the pass rush.

But let's admit it. On a third and twelve situation, the secondary will be thinking "pass," and the defensive line will be thinking "sack." So

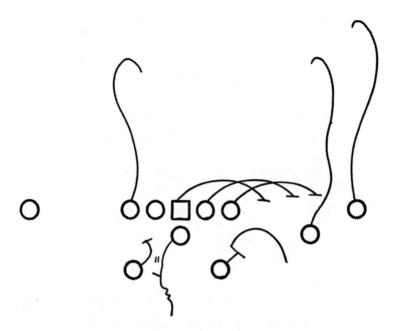

Figure 10-27 "Open Pro Spread right/Fake draw/Screen right"

dropback action is the answer. But to minimize the effects of quick defensive penetration, we often predetermine a quarterback scramble.

Recognizing that most defensive linemen—with the exception of the outside contain men, usually the defensive ends—will accept an invitation to rush to the inside, we instruct the line to take them that way. After the quarterback drops and sets up, he holds for one count, then sprints out quickly to the outside on a scramble move. The backs provide a moving screen for him. The center, if uncovered, drops to pick up any backside rush.

Obviously, we also can just roll out or sprint out in either direction, but we've discovered that the predetermined scramble enables us to predict a better-contained pass rush. The line likes it because they enjoy the option of inviting the defensive line to take a more predictable path to the quarterback.

A final few suggestions. Against man-to-man coverage in the secondary, try as much as possible to run crossing patterns, such as the Alabama, the Florida, and the Eastern. Against zone or combo coverage, delay ends or backs out of the backfield as much as possible, particularly if you can give the backs the chance to swing sharp into a hook zone vacated by a linebacker. This strategy requires a quarterback with a quick release, but most of the quarterbacks we've had have been able to handle it.

Finally, don't forget the fake draw screen as illustrated in figure 10-27. We like to spread out the defense as much as possible when we execute the play, so we designate it "Open Pro Spread Right/Drop back/Fake draw-screen right." The player involved in the fake draw is always the player away from the screen.

The fake is executed much like the deep power fake on play action, and the line is instructed to help matters along by shouting "Draw," much as they shout "Counter," on our counter-action passes. We're nothing if not helpful.

Well, we hope this chapter has been helpful to you. Remember, if it is to work for you, you'll have to coordinate it very carefully with your running attack. And *most* important, you'll have to establish a mind set that allows you to throw on first and second downs. That is perhaps the single most important element in a sophisticated play-action passing attack.

11

Tricks of the Trade

We all know that an occasional break from the routine, no matter how short, clears out the cobwebs and gets our goals in sharper focus, particularly if the break is fun. New moms find a welcomed escape from the little one(s) by attacking the local salad bar with a friend. Business executives abandon their mahogany desks for an occasional frolic on the sun-warmed sands of the South Seas. And we break away from the dizzying array of Xs and Os by pushing out onto Lake Kenaugesaga and wiggling a minnow in front of the Great American Walleye.

Players need a break, too. Like you, we devote time in meetings and on the field justifying the time we devote to drills. The repetition a good drill provides may weary even the most dedicated kid on the field, but it also provokes the necessary kinesthetic conditioning an athlete requires to execute his assignments smoothly.

But drill after drill, scrimmage after scrimmage wears thin after a while, so we disrupt the tedium occasionally by introducing a little something new. It doesn't take much time, and it usually gives the players an opportunity to do something different, to display a new skill or to surprise the opponent.

No, we're not talking about the "huddle-screen" or one of several "far out" offensive alignments. They usually take too much time to refine, and we expect that we would hit a point of diminishing returns before we realized any kind of pay off. So we avoid the *real* "Park district" stuff, although one of our toughest opponents almost beat us late in the game one year with a huddle screen. He would have pulled it off, too, except that one of his kids went offside. Such, however, is the inherent problem with the huddle screen. *Live* by the huddle screen; *die* by the ... !

THE END AROUND

But we *do* like the end around, *and* the end around pass to both sides, assuming we have an end who can throw the ball. We normally have little trouble finding one. Most ends spent every waking hour of their childhoods tossing a football around their backyards. Certainly they had

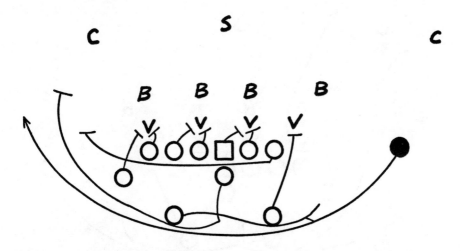

Figure 11-1 "Pro 7 Split/Power end reverse at 7"

more fun catching the ball; that's why they decided to become ends. But somewhere along the way they learned to throw, too.

So we take advantage of their skills by calling the "Pro 7 Split/Power end reverse at 7," as illustrated in figure 11-1. Against the 4-4 stack, as diagrammed, the play provides two-team blocks along the line of scrimmage and in effect disregards the linebackers, who are likely to go with backfield flow.

Obviously, we can't maintain a steady diet of such plays, but when the time is right and we get the urge, this kind of misdirection is as good as any. It eliminates inside penetration and takes away the attack defense's strategy against counter or reverse action. It also provides two lead blockers for the end, who receives an outside hand off from the running back.

That's the running play. It serves as the foundation for two excellent pass plays, the first of which is illustrated in figure 11-2. The play is fundamentally the same as the running play, with the exception of the left end and the right tackle. The tackle doesn't pull, and the left end blocks for three full counts before releasing on his pass route. It's a one-man pattern. It took us a long time, but we've finally accepted the fact that one-man patterns are devastating with play action, particularly if it involves misdirection.

That's why the third play in the sequence has been so good for us. After our opponents have had time to scout us and to incorporate their keys for this sequence into their game plan, we like to call the "Pro 7 Split/Fake end around pass." Illustrated in figure 11-3, the play has resulted in several gamebreakers over the years.

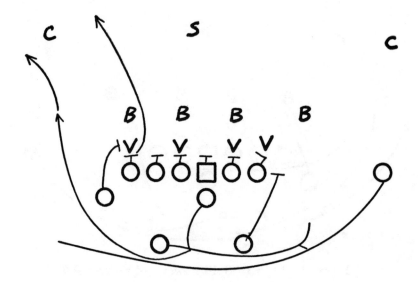

Figure 11-2 "Pro 7 Split/Power end reverse pass at 7"

After making a cursory fake to the split end, the running back tucks in the ball, takes three hard steps to the outside, and looks for the tight end running his diagonal across the field. This, too, is a one-man pattern and puts real heat on the linebackers and secondary. But what we like about the whole sequence is its ability to equalize the attack capability of the defense and to have a little fun while we're doing it.

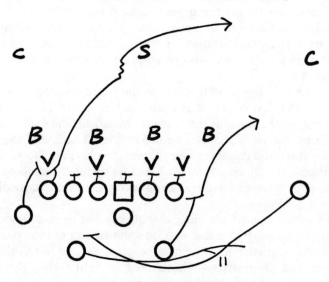

Figure 11-3 "Pro 7 Split/Fake end around pass"

PLAYING OUTSIDE

Another play that provides some quick excitement for both us and the fans is the "Pro 6/Quick pitch at 8." Any quick-pitch play is a gamble. That's why it's not a basic play in our offense, but the play's ability to attack the relatively weak containment capability of a defense like the 4-4 stack makes it worth the risk. Figure 11-4 illustrates the play's exceptional ability to attack the outside, particularly against the outside man on defense who has been instructed to jam the end whenever he down-blocks.

Obviously, it can do the same thing to any even defensive front as well as to the 5-2. The Pro 6 set keeps the defense tight, tighter than it is for teams that run the play to a wingback's side. So we instruct the setback to release hard to the outside and to shield block the player in the outside tandem to assume outside responsibility.

The onside end releases to the linebacker, and the right guard seals on. The left halfback, after taking a fake from the quarterback, has the primary responsibility of cutting off any kind of penetration through the off-tackle hole. After pitching the ball and making the fake to the left halfback, the quarterback drops back as if to pass the ball.

As evidenced in figure 11-5, the "Pro 6/Fake quick pitch/Slant at 6" is an excellent complement to the outside play, particularly with the setback in the six hole. His positioning gives us a double-team block on the defensive tackle, the most dangerous man to the play's success. The key block, however, comes from our right tackle, who has the responsibility of shield blocking the man in the outside tandem to come to the inside.

If he does an effective job, the play will work, because we're not concerned with the other player in the inside tandem. He is likely to be

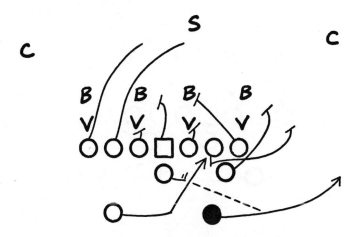

Figure 11-4 "Pro 6/Quick pitch at 8"

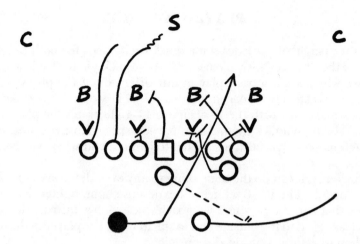

Figure 11-5 "Pro 6/Fake Quick pitch/Slant at 6"

preoccupied with the fake quick pitch. Again, the key to the play's success is the setback's double-team block and our ability to influence the outside man without having to block him. Those strategies represent two of our most effective principles against attack defenses: use the double-team block to neutralize their unpredictability, and don't block the player who doesn't need to be blocked.

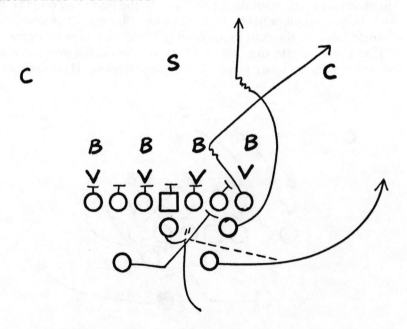

Figure 11-6 "Pro 6/quick pitch pass at 8"

The final complement within the quick-pitch sequence is the "Pro 6/Quick pitch pass," as illustrated in figure 11-6. Again, the pass releases are consistent with the blocking action, making the pass play especially effective against an overanxious secondary fill. If the cornerback comes up hard when he sees the quick-pitch fake or the fake to the left halfback, the play is a gainer.

Even if the cornerback is only immobilized, he is unable to handle the flood action in his zone. Again, the play capitalizes on the principle of variable penetration into the secondary. The setback is instructed to release hard to stalk the safety and then to break deep behind him. The end is to down-block for just one count, then release hard into the cornerback's area. He usually is the player who is most open on the play.

ON THE MOVE

We have discovered, however, that the *best* way to get players open is to use motion. Motion is strategy in action. We have known few coaches who use motion to camouflage their intended strategies. Most coaches make known their intentions immediately by shifting or motioning from one formation to another to gain strategic advantage over the defense.

As we all know, however, motion doesn't provide a lot of time for defenses to make the adjustments they need to compensate for the offensive team's sudden strategic advantage. That's why we like it against attack defenses—and not for the simple reason that it gives us a numerical advantage to one side of the formation.

Like all good defensive coaches, the coach of the attack defense works long and hard scouting his opponent's tendencies and adjusting his stunts to stop them. Given the variety of stunts that he is likely to deploy, he certainly has worked out his own special lexicon for calling them, and he has identified the player on the defensive team who will translate the signals from the sidelines into a call in the huddle.

That's where motion comes in for the offensive coach. Not only does motion provide the relatively basic strategic advantage of creating an offensive overload somewhere along the line of scrimmage, but it confounds the calls of the attack defense by confronting them with a formation that is different—sometimes significantly—from the one they were prepared for.

Motion, therefore, provides much more than numerical advantage. It creates new tendencies; it obviates certain linebacker blitzes and forces their realignment; it forces the secondary to change its coverage; it creates man-to-man coverage on key receivers; it redirects the thrust of the offense; and it generally forces the defense to doubt the efficiency of their game plan.

Here's how we do it. Our use of motion isn't unique. It is different

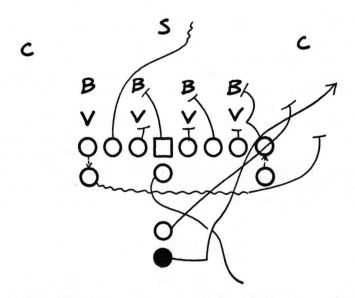

Figure 11-7 I8/Leer/Deep Power Right"

only to the extent that its design is uniquely suited to our offense. For
example, figure 11-7 illustrates an "I 8/Leer (left end motion right)/ Deep
Power right." The word "Leer" instructs the left ends to take a step
forward when the quarterback says "Down." When the quarterback raises
his heel (the signal that starts all our motion), the tight end executes flat
motion behind the quarterback.

Obviously, the timing is critical if the motioned end is to be in the
right spot to lead the play around the end when the ball is snapped.
The play is illustrated versus the 4-4 stack because we like a motioned
tight end against the relatively weak containment capability of the 4-4.
The wingback causes it *enough* trouble, but when we bring him up on
the line of scrimmage to give him an angle block on the outside man,
the defense is in *real* trouble.

The wingback is instructed to two-team the down lineman in the outside stack—unless he slants away into the end/tackle gap. If the down
lineman slants away, the wingback is told to plateau to the linebacker
and either shoulder or shield block him until he gets some help.

The play can be overpowering, especially if only the secondary adjusts
to motion. Given the fact, however, that we are creating an unbalanced
line with the motion, normally the linebackers have to make some kind
of an adjustment. The backer in the outside tandem may realign himself
as in figure 11-8, in which case the end and repositioned wingback will
cross-block the outside. The motioned end, looking for the defensive

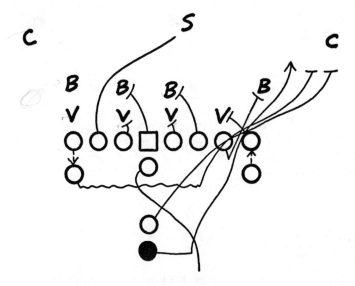

Figure 11-8

adjustment while executing his motion, will expect to lead the play through the point of attack.

The right tackle still has his angle block on the inside linebacker; in effect, we have overloaded the point of attack once again. Obviously the defense won't tolerate that very long, so they might adjust by sliding the linebackers over a man into the motioned side of the offensive formation.

KING LEER

Our reaction, then, will be to hit back to the weakside of the formation with the "I 8/Leer/Deep Power counter at 5," as diagrammed in figure 11-9. Even if the play is only moderately successful, we must remember that we nevertheless have accomplished a very important adjustment in the defensive alignment. They've been chased out of their 4-4 stack, their favorite defense. Now we can run the I 8/Leer with all the rest of our plays: cross fire action up the middle, inside belly, etc.

Leer isn't the *only* successful motion. We also like several others. Figure 11-10 provides the names and the motions they involve. Our other motion from the wingback positions are simply designated either "motion right" or "flat motion right" and usually are executed in the direction of the play — although not necessarily.

We get a lot of mileage from the "fill" and "far" motions. Figure 11-11 illustrates the "Pro 10/Fill/Power at 6" versus the 4-4. All we're doing

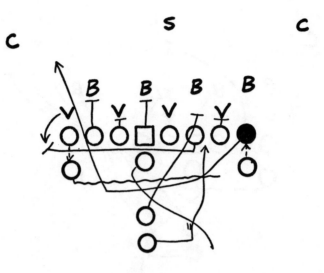

Figure 11-9

is motioning the flanker back to the four set and running our regular power play. We can do the same thing with other backfield alignments in order to run effective "lead" plays from our other series.

We also can motion the flanker back to a modified wing position in order to pick on the safety. Figure 11-12 illustrates the "Pro 10/Fill/Power right/Guards." The play puts the flanker in motion and, instead of bringing him all the way back to a six or a four set, puts him directly onto the safety, who is likely to have an inside-out fill responsibility on any action in or outside of the off-tackle hole. Both guards provide good protection to the outside, and the onside end's down-blocking responsibility probably will cause the defensive man to jam the off-tackle hole, setting up the fullback's block.

LEER	Left End motion Right
LOLL	Left End motion Left
ROAR	Right End motion Right
RAIL	Right End motion Left
FILL	Flanker motion Left
FAR	Flanker motion Right
SOLE	Split End motion Left
SORE	Split End motion Right
HIRE	Halfback motion Right
HEEL	Halfback motion Left

Figure 11-10

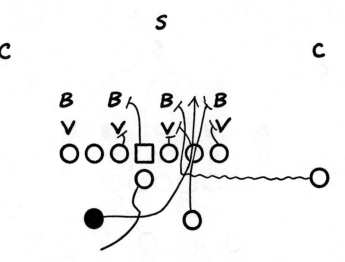

Figure 11-11 "Pro 10/Fill/Power at 6"

The key to the play, however, is the motioned flanker's stalk block on the safety. Because the safety is going to be conscious of his fill responsibility and because most safeties enjoy running into their fellow man anyway, he is likely to try to stick his nose into the action as soon as he reads the end's down block.

That's why the flanker must sprint to an area about three yards in front of the safety as soon as the ball is snapped. Then he must assume

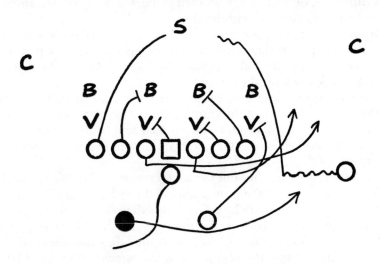

Figure 11-12 "Pro 10/Fill/Power Right Guards"

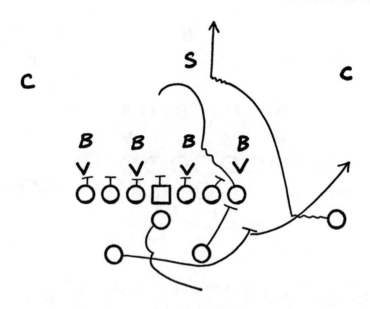

Figure 11-13 "Pro 10/Fill/Power right action/Power pass"

his "hit position," stalk the safety, and cut him down or shield him when he tries to get into the action.

A good blocker realizes that his block on the safety doesn't have to be devastating. The crowd may enjoy real head knockers, but coaches are usually satisfied with any effort that keeps the safety off the ball carrier. Toughness is essential in any football game, but it won't guarantee victories unless it's coupled with brains.

"Brains" also tell a good pass "deceiver" that an effective stalk block on a running play is the perfect way to set up a safety on a play-action pass. Figure 11-13 illustrates the same play capitalizing on the motioned flanker's stalk block on the safety.

The motion man executes exactly the same kind of stalk maneuver on the safety as he did on the running play. The right end aggressively blocks the man on his head, trying to take him to the inside, and the fullback aggressively blocks the player on the tandem who assumes outside responsibility.

If they execute their fire-out blocks aggressively, the safety is likely to believe that the play is a run, particularly if the motioned flanker executes a convincing stalk block on him. Once the safety starts to fill or goes flat-footed because of indecision, the motion man should break past him and run a diagonal toward the flag. Both the safety and the cornerback will be sucked up into the play action if the linemen do a good sell job and the motion man has the patience to force the safety's hand.

MORE MOTION

The pass play from power action with motion, particularly when run with a one-man pattern, has been unbelievably wide open for us in the past. Obviously, much of the play's success is dependent on the skills of the flanker back. That's why so much of our time during practice is devoted to proper execution. But it pays dividends.

Consider the dividends against the attack defense that employs a three-deep secondary. Motion can force linebacker coverage on one of your fastest backs and, perhaps, best pass receivers. Figure 11-14 illustrates

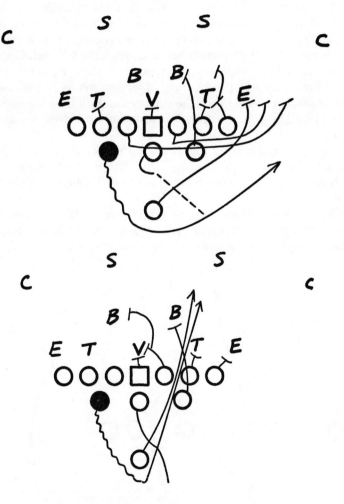

Figure 11-14 "I3-4/Motion/Power at 4"
"I3-4/Motion/Sweep at 8"

an "Open I spread right" formation with tailback motion left, followed by a fly pattern into the secondary.

Notice first that the formation has divided the secondary and that the patterns of each of the wide receivers are designed to occupy each of the defenders, in effect forcing the outside backer to cover the tailback deep. If used in a big game, before the defense establishes your tendency, this particular strategy is very effective.

If your left end is your good receiver, you might want to modify the strategy as illustrated in figure 11-15. The formation call is "I spread right," and the play is designated "Tailback motion left/Quickie pass left." The defensive left cornerback and safety probably will be using some kind of combo defense on the spread side of the formation.

The right cornerback, therefore, is the likely player to take the tailback when he motions left. No one is home to cover the left end. Good attack defenses will jam the tight end, particularly if they've scouted this play. If they haven't, it could be big. It could be big anyway. We all know how often our players forget to jam the end, especially if they are unprepared for the play. The spread formation with motion provides that kind of strategic edge.

So does the double wing formation with motion. We've indicated in an earlier chapter that it gives us virtually our entire offense without providing any tendencies by formation. And the motion is not difficult to time.

Neither is motion from the I 34 set. Figure 11-16 illustrates the I 34 with motion right and a power play, then a complementary sweep. The motion is simple. It's the basic principle that counts.

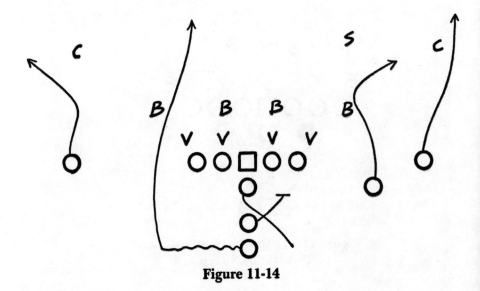

Figure 11-14

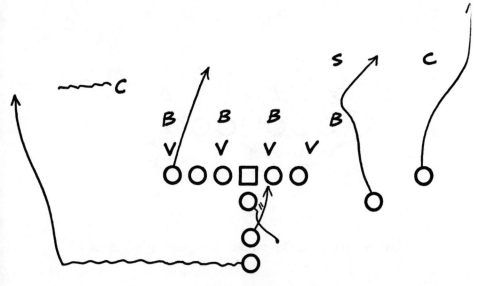

Figure 11-15

The same thing is true of almost every kind of motion. The important point to be emphasized is that each of us should take the time to work on it, perhaps as hard as we work on the execution of our most important plays. Too often we overlook the strategic effectiveness of motion to confuse defensive calls and to force defensive realignment. To most coaches it represents icing on the cake, an appetizing but unsatisfying bit of fluff that doesn't justify the time spent on it.

To us, it represents an easily installed element of strategy that pays dividends far in excess of the time invested. It complements our offense and incorporates an element of surprise that most attack defenses would like to avoid. It just stands to reason that a defense that makes all its calls based on the offensive alignment doesn't want that alignment to change or to do anything unpredictable.

So we call plays such as the "T 8/Flat motion left/Quick quarterback keep at 7." We will call it, certainly, after we've established a pattern of our own tendencies from the T 8 formation. Because some teams maintain a strong focus on down and distance tendencies as well as formation tendencies, we scout both in ourselves and then use motion to change the formation and the point of attack.

For example, assume that the defense has determined that on first and ten, we have run 32 plays—6 pass, 26 run—and that 23 of the 26 were run between our tackles. On that basis, they decide to move the tackles inside on the odd-man front and to overshift the linebackers to the strength of the formation as in figure 11-17. This is only one of several possible attack sets they might use, but, like the others, it focuses

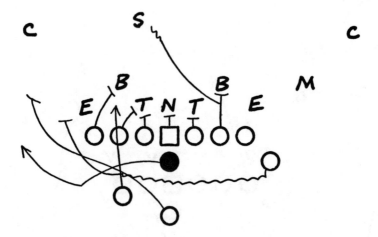

Figure 11-17 "T8/Flat motion left/Quick QB keep at 7"

on stopping our cross fire action up the gut or any of our quick-hitting plays to the left halfback.

But if we've done our homework and have scouted ourselves to determine the same tendency, we can invite them into their inside attack mode by setting up initially in a T 8. Then we will motion out of it by using flat motion, overload the left side of the offensive formation, and break the inside tendency by running the quarterback at 7.

Or we can simply run the fullback at 5 as in figure 11-18. We like to

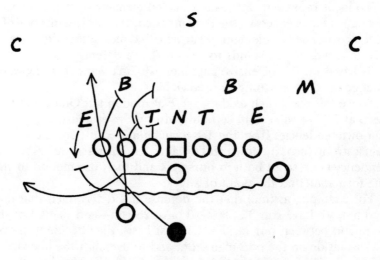

Figure 11-18 "T8/Flat motion left/Quick at 5"

run our quarterback because it gives us one more blocker, but if your fullback is one of your best ball carriers, give the ball to him. The important point is to break the offensive tendency. Given the fact that we may be unfamiliar with the scouting format of each opponent, it's always wise to chart your own tendencies based on down and distance, formation, and field position.

All that, however, will be discussed in the next chapter.

LET'S WRAP IT UP

Motion in most any offensive attack at any level of football generally is a late arrival. Young, developing programs usually are too busy organizing the offense and establishing the fundamentals of execution to find the time to integrate motion into their weekly game plan. It was a late arrival in our program as well. It took us several years to become comfortable with what we were doing offensively before we felt confident enough to add motion to our attack.

Most programs have trouble enough just figuring out a way to designate their plays and to communicate them during the game from sidelines to huddle without further complicating communication by adding one of several different kinds of motion to the play call. Our format works because it's easy to remember and because it covers most of the kinds of motion we like to use on game days.

On those few occasions when we decide to use yo-yo motion or fake motion or to put the fullback in motion, we simply call the play as "yo-yo motion left" or "false motion right." Similarly, when we run our regular motion from the wing or double wing, we simply call "motion;" the direction of the play will instruct the appropriate wingback to go in motion. If the play involves flat motion, we designate it accordingly.

The important thing to remember is that it pays dividends to establish your own designation format. It doesn't take as much time, and it provides a whole new dimension to your offensive attack without confusing your players and without adding significant amounts of time to your practice sessions.

As a matter of fact, the inclusion of motion into your offensive attack is likely to add more time to your opponent's practice time than it is to yours, particularly if your opponent uses an attack defense. They're going to have to adjust their defenses as well as their play-calling patterns in order to feel any confidence in their game plan.

As indicated already in this chapter, most attack defenses have worked long and hard to establish your offensive tendencies, and they want to establish their defensive calls based on down and distance, formation, and sometimes field position. If you show one formation, let them make their play call, and motion into another formation or *shift* into another, the defense grows uncomfortable.

That's one reason why shifting in the backfield can be another very effective strategy. We have consciously excluded backfield shifting because of the amount of time it would require to do it justice in this chapter. It isn't that we don't use it or that we don't believe in it. We'll also admit that we don't use it as often as we use motion, but we're quick to acknowledge that, combined with motion, backfield shifting can further complicate the problems for attack defenses.

It seems the key to using motion and to shifting in the backfield involves a comprehensive program of not only scouting your opponents but also *yourself*. It's important that we understand our own tendencies in order to break those patterns, particularly in the big games against our toughest opponents.

We feel that our self-scouting format is as good as we've seen, so it will become the focus of the next chapter.

12

Scouting Yourself: Seeing Ourselves As Others See Us

Taking a good, hard look at oneself never hurt anybody. Psychologists advise us to occasionally introspect; poet Bobby Burns years ago advised: "O wad some Power the giftie gie us to see oursels as ithers see us!" If any of us is to change for the better, it's advisable for us to take two or three steps backward and take a close look at what we're doing. As important as that principle is to each of us personally, it is *as* important to each of us coaches. Burns' next line tells us, and we paraphrase: "It would from many a blunder free us."

That's what self-scouting accomplishes. It frees us from many blunders. Each of us may picture ourselves in many different ways, just as each of us, as coach, pictures our programs in a variety of ways. But we can be assured of one thing: our individuality may be important to us, but in most respects we are amazingly like everyone else.

Applied to coaching, that saying suggests that we each have individual preferences; we tend to favor one side of the offensive formation over the other; and we usually fall into predictable patterns of play calls. Psychologists tell us, for example, that in stressful situations, human beings regress to previously learned behaviors. What that means in coaching lexicon is that in a tight situation in a game, each of us is likely to call plays that have been successful for us in the past.

The problem for us is that our opponents realize that just as much as we do. They are likely to be looking for those plays. In order to avoid the trap, therefore, it is essential that we take those three steps backward in order to make the determination of exactly what we're doing—at a time when we're not stressed and are able to make a reasoned response to each of our observed tendencies.

171

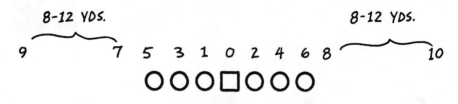

Figure 12-1

KEEPING IT SIMPLE

To develop a good scouting system—for yourself or for your opponents—it is important to start from a good base, one that keeps it simple. Our base is as simple, yet as effective, as we have seen. It involves a base of ten. We identify ten positions along the line of scrimmage and number them, starting with the smallest numbers in the middle of the line and working out toward the widest men in the formation.

As illustrated in figure 12-1, the left guard is numbered one, the right guard 2, the left tackle 3, the right tackle 4, the left end 5, and the right end 6. Positions 7 and 8 are occupied by wingbacks; and positions 9 and 10, located 8 to 12 yards outside the tight end, are occupied by the flanker backs.

We also can slot the backs by designating them in the 5 or 6 positions. As indicated in earlier chapters, we can also position our backs in the 3 and 4 slots. We can even put them in the one and two slots, although this strategy is rare.

The process for positioning our ends is equally simple. To split the left end, we initiate the formation call with the word "open." When we split our right end, we *conclude* the formation call with the word "split." In essence, then, our formation call moves from left to right, starting with the left end if we want to position him in anything other than his tight end location.

If we want our left end positioned three to five yards outside the offensive left tackle, we initiate the formation call with the word "flex." If we want our right end similarly positioned, we *conclude* the formation call with the word "flex."

POSITIONING THE BACKS

Our entire offense is executed from five basic backfield alignments. Figure 12-2 illustrates the pro alignment, which is typically the professional backfield alignment; the wing, which overloads the backfield to one side of our formation; the T, which positions the wingback to the

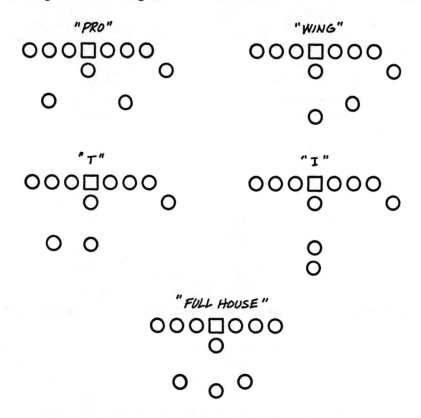

Figure 12-2 "Pro" "Wing" "T" "I" "Full House"

side away from the home halfback; the I, which for us normally involves a wingback or a slotback; and the full house, which we use surprisingly often because of the balance it provides.

Recall that from the Pro, Wing, T, and I formations, although we normally use a wingback, we will position the setback in the 3, 4, 5, or 6 positions, particularly against attack defenses. We can run from the wishbone or the shotgun; normally, however, we restrict ourselves to one of the five alignments illustrated in figure 12-2.

So, when we combine the varying backfield alignments with the numbering system along the line of scrimmage, we find it easy to designate one of hundreds of possible offensive formations. Figure 12-3 illustrates several examples. For what might be a mouthful for some programs, our formation calling is short and descriptive.

For example, if the offensive team wants to split the left end, run from a pro/deuce backfield, and flanker the right halfback, it may bury itself in a deluge of unnecessary verbiage. All we do is call an "open/Pro

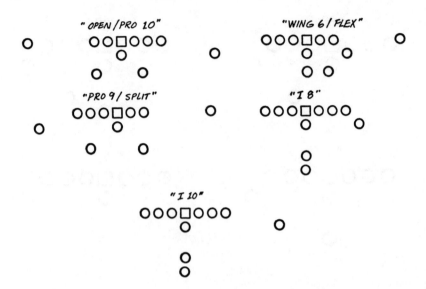

Figure 12-3 "Open/Pro 10" "Pro 9/Split" "I8" "I10" "Wing6/Flex"

10." If we wanted to reverse the formation in order to put our left halfback and our right end into deep patterns, we would call the formation a "Pro 9/Split." Again, the formation call moves from left to right. If the ends are to remain in their tight end positions, we don't instruct them with the call. Only the players involved are instructed by the formation call.

If, for example, we want both ends to remain tight, but we want the right halfback to go to the wing and the remaining backs to align themselves in an I set, we call the formation an "I 8." In essence, that's it. Figure 12-4 illustrates and names several more variations. We can run from the double wing, the shotgun, the spread and double spread, but they are easy enough to call without trying to modify our system.

The formation-calling system is very simple — yet very comprehensive. It's easily learned by the players and communicated to them during a game, and it provides us a very solid foundation for scouting our opponents as well as for scouting ourselves.

THE PLAY-CALLING SYSTEM: MAINTAINING THE SIMPLICITY

The numbered positions along the line of scrimmage are also essential within our play-calling format. We utilize several different series within our offense attack: the Quick series, the Cross fire series, the inside belly series, the outside belly series, the power series, and the sweep.

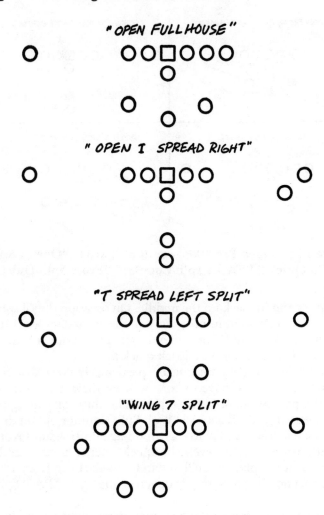

Figure 12-4 "Open Full House" "Open I Spread Right"
"T spread left split" "Win 7 Split"

Because the combination of those series represents the accumulation of what most teams do offensively, we simply use them in combination with our numbering system to describe the opponent's plays. Figure 12-5, for example, illustrates four popular plays run by most teams and describes each within our terminology.

The first of the four illustrates one of Vince Lombardi's old standbys, the power sweep. We would simply designate the play an "Open/Pro 10—Power at 8/Guards." For teams that like to run their tailback out of the I formation, an effective sequence for them is a quick opener or a

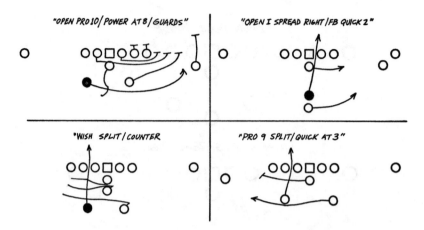

Figure 12-5 "Open Pro 10/Power at 8/Guards" "Open I Spread Right/FB Quick 2" "Wish Split/Counter" "Pro 9 Split/Quick at 3"

short trap for the fullback up the middle. On occasion they'll spread out their offensive formation in order to pull the secondary away from the point of attack. We would simply identify the play in our scouting report as an "Open I spread Right/Fullback quick at 2."

For the teams that get a bit fancier, particularly those that run from the wishbone, we might have to borrow from their lexicon in order to describe the play in our scouting report. The third play in figure 12-5, therefore, would be designated a "Wish Split/Counter option dive at 3."

As a final example, a play that is an on-again-off-again favorite of a good many teams at any level, the quick opener to the halfback or fullback is as basic a play as you'll find in football. If run from a standard pro set formation, we would simply designate the play a "Pro 9 Split/Quick at 3."

Our formation-calling system accommodates almost any kind of offensive set, and our play-calling format provides a name for almost any kind of play run by our opponents. For those few plays that may be new to us, we simply devise a name for them and/or diagram the play on the margin of the scouting report. But that doesn't happen very often, because we've discovered over the years that our format accommodates almost anything our opponents do.

So, let's assume for the moment that the deep green of summer is giving way to the reds and burnished oranges of fall, and we're sitting delicately on the edge of a stadium seat trying to balance all those sheets of paper that constitute our scouting report. Obviously, we want to get all of their kicking game, the numbers and sizes of their personnel, the names of their best athletes, their basic defenses and adjustments, and the wealth of additional information that provides that necessary "feel" for what they do.

THE FORMAT

But for the offensive coach, the most important of all those papers is the one illustrated in figure 12-6. It contains all the information we need to determine our opponent's tendencies based on field position, down and distance, formation, and even the frequency of one player carrying the ball.

For purposes of illustration, we've provided six random plays, four running, and two passing. Let's assume that we are out scouting and that our opponent has executed these plays, perhaps several times. Figure 12-6 represents each of the plays in verbal form, the composite of which will yield his tendencies.

As you can tell, the format accommodates field position, down and distance, formation, play call, ball carrier, and yardage gained. We have the opportunity, therefore, to feed into the computer specific information that will yield three tendencies: field position (we can designate left or right hash in the box provided), formation, and down and distance.

The remainder of the format enables us to identify the play, the amount of yardage gained—in essence the success they have had with

Field Position	Down and Distance	Formation	Play Call	Ball Carrier	Yardage Gained
ND10 left hash	1–10	OI10	P (ower) 6	23	+3
ND13 left hash	2–7	OI10	P trap 4	23	+7
ND20 midfield	1–10	I9S	IB3	33	+5
ND25 midfield	2–5	Pro 8	P counter at 5	18	+18
ND43 right hash	1–10	OI spd rgt.	XF12T	33	+6
ND49 right hash	2–4	Pro 8	P right action flood pass	see pass sheet	Inc.

Figure 12-6

each play—and the ball carrier. This latter piece of information can also yield a valuable insight. Given the numbers of teams who run their tailback thirty times per game, opposing coaches don't have too tough a time identifying the favorite ball carrier.

A bit more subtle, however, is the tendency of some offensive teams to run their favorite ball carrier behind their favorite tandem of blockers at important parts of the game. Similarly, many coaches, ourselves included, tend to run certain players at predictable times in the game—first and ten, third and short. Add that tendency to formation tendencies, and defensive coaches can write the book on what their opponents like to do.

Again, that's the big reason why we take the same format and apply it to ourselves every week. One of our assistant coaches is able to chart our tendencies. He doesn't have to watch for nuances within the play. We can fill that in when someone pumps the information into the computer. All we want are the basics. We can take that good, hard look at ourselves with just that.

After we have accumulated several scouting reports on either our

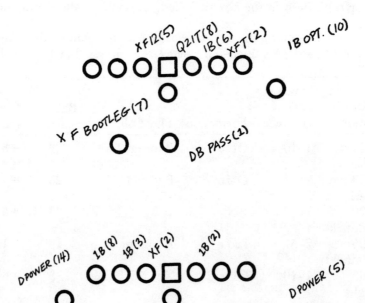

Figure 12-7

opponents or ourselves, we like to break down the information graph-ically. We break it down on a formation-by-formation basis in order to gain a clearer understanding of what we or our opponents are doing offensively.

Figure 12-7 provides an example of what the final result looks like. With such information available to us, we gain a much clearer under-standing of how we try to win ball games. We also find ourselves able to predict with greater certainty what our opponents are likely to try to do to stop us.

We also will use our down and distance tendencies, as illustrated in figure 12-8. We've discovered over the years that our down and distance tendencies and our formation tendencies are very similar. The combi-nation of the two gives us a vivid picture of the predictability we are developing. One tendency chart seems to substantiate the other tendency chart, so we feel pretty comfortable with the offensive adjustments we make.

This, however, is not a book on defense, so we won't discuss defensive adjustments. The thrust of this chapter is to sell you on the need to scout *yourself* and then to make whatever *offensive* adjustments you have to make in order to negate the opponent's defensive strategies.

COUNTERING THE ATTACK

Now let's assume that we have done a good job scouting ourselves and have discovered that we have established the pronounced tendencies evidenced in figure 12-7. While running from the T formation, for example, we observed that we ran between the tackles most of the time, and our down and distance chart indicated that on first and ten we ran between the tackles fifteen of the twenty times we ran the ball.

We've observed that we tend to run our fullback on first and ten with cross fire at one or twelve action a large percentage of the time. We also run the cross fire trap at four as a complement or the quick at 3 to the left halfback.

We have several ways to go. First of all, we can assume that our op-ponent is as familiar with these tendencies as we are. So he's going to do whatever he can to capitalize on that knowledge.

So are we. We will wait for the big game, therefore, and instead of running between the tackles from the T 8 on first and ten, we'll run the "T 8/Cross fire Counter at 5" as illustrated in figure 12-8. Or we'll run the "T 8/Quick quarterback Keep at 7" as in figure 12-9. Or we'll cap-italize on one of our earlier principles and hit the area(s) vacated by the linebackers by running a "T 8/Cross fire at 8 action/Right Alabama" as diagrammed in figure 12-10.

1–10 (156)

Within tackles   –92 times
Left end   –10 times
Right end   –26 times
DB pass   – 2 times
Bootleg pass   –12 times
Play-action   –14 times

2nd–short (87)

Within tackles   –72 times
Left end   – 6 times
Right end   – 5 times
Play action pass– 4 times

2nd–long (69)

Within tackles   –22 times
Left end   –20 times
Right end   –16 times
DB pass   – 5 times
Screen left   – 4 times
Play action pass– 2 times

3rd–short
3rd–long

Figure 12-8

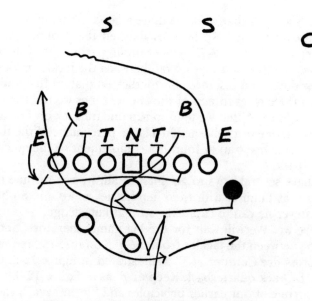

Figure 12-8 "T8/XF counter at 5"

180

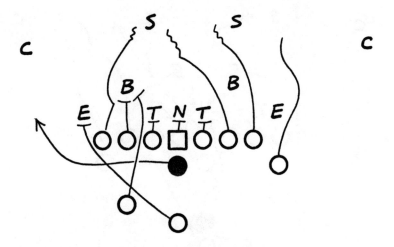

Figure 12-9 "T8/Quick QB keep at 7"

We can do the same thing from the I formation. If the Deep Power is the obvious tendency, particularly on second or third down situations, we can invite the defense to attack the off-tackle holes and run up the gut with the "I 8/Cross fire at 12 trap" as in figure 12-11 or the "I 8/Power at 2" as in figure 12-12.

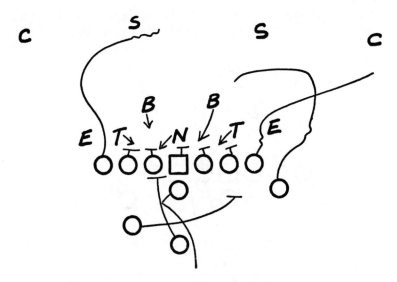

Figure 12-10 "T8/XF 8 action/Right Alabama"

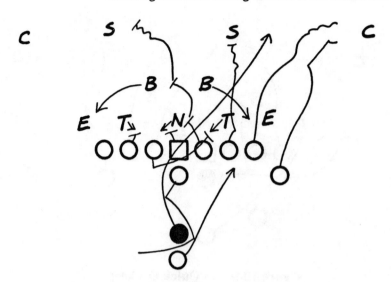

Figure 12-11 "I8/XF 12 Trap"

There are a lot of things you can do to break your tendencies, all of which are contingent on the kind of offense you run, *or* on your willingness to borrow from folks like us. But again, the critical issue centers on our knowledge of what those tendencies *are* before we devise ways to break them.

This leads to another point. Normally, we begin to break our tendencies about a third of the way through the season, depending on the

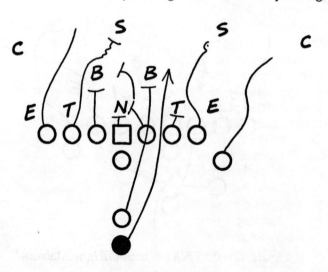

12-12 "I8/Power 2"

relative difficulty of the schedule at that time. By that time, we've probably established a pretty consistent pattern of formation and play-calling. We can break them during the fourth or fifth game, depending on the team we are going to play. Or we can let them ride, actually *maintain* them in order to set up our toughest opponent(s).

The important thing is to have the tendency charts on hand each week in order to be able to break the tendencies when the time is right. It may be the fourth game of the season or the last. That depends on the talents of your opponents. But when the time *does* come, it is important to establish the same tendencies with complementary plays.

LET'S WRAP IT UP

This chapter could have enumerated a score of tendencies and tendency-breaking plays, but the primary focus of the chapter is *how to determine* those tendencies and to encourage you to break them within the framework of your offense.

Having established your tendencies, you can do one of two things. We can take a page from Vince Lombardi's book and run our plays regardless *what* the defense does to try to stop them. Or, two, we can establish our tendencies, document them, and then break them at critical times during the season.

We prefer to keep track of our tendencies and then break them during the season, particularly against an attack defense that likes to load up at strategic points along the line of scrimmage. Certainly we have discovered, as you have, that few of us are blessed with the kind of personnel that Lombardi used on his power sweep.

Give us a Jerry Kramer and a Fuzzy Thurston to lead our power plays and the essential tendency we'll show is to win. We do that pretty much anyway, given the fact that we do our homework.

The obvious guidelines when doing that homework involve our running from the same formations and inviting the defense to stunt into relatively predictable patterns, certainly more predictable than if we had not scouted ourselves. Then, we run plays designed to capitalize on the expected stunts. We don't necessarily expect that the defense will exhibit weaknesses in certain spots, although they sometimes do. More important, we like to determine likely stunts in order to develop effective blocking schemes.

Exactly how you do this depends on the flexibility of your offensive system and the unique and collective talents of your players. For the last time, you'll be able to do it much more effectively if you maintain a handle on what you've been doing offensively up to that point in the season. As we've indicated already, the format described in this chapter is as good as anybody's.

Borrow part of it or take all of it. It is so concise that it can be handled by a single coach on a scouting assignment. Obviously, we don't like to send one coach to scout an opponent, but there are times of the year (before play offs, when we are scouting several likely opponents) when we have no alternative. At such times, we realize renewed respect for our scouting format. It's made to order for any school but particularly for small schools with a limited number of coaches.

You can be sure that the nation's major universities are well aware of their own tendencies. As we both know, it's not beyond a great program to establish certain tendencies against weaker opponents in order to break them against stronger opponents. With that thought in mind, let's take a look at two of the nation's finest.

We have good friends at each school and were able to borrow from each of them to illustrate our points further. Fortunately, they substantiate everything we have said so far, so let's conclude the book with a look at the universities of Wisconsin and Notre Dame.

13

Notre Dame and Wisconsin: What They Do

How about clearing up a popular misconception? Attack defenses do not devote their pregame preparation to frenzied dances around an early-evening bonfire. Nor do they attack the line of scrimmage with the blind abandon of Sitting Bull's shock troops. To the contrary, they devote hours and hours to the objective analysis of opponents' tendencies, to the organization of the appropriate combination of stunts to stop those tendencies, to a game plan that makes every attempt to ensure the proper pursuit paths, and essentially to the development of a strategically patterned network of defensive maneuvers designed to stop almost any kind of running and passing attack.

Similarly, the players are expected to penetrate deliberately into predetermined gaps to confuse blocking schemes and to create a pile at the point of attack. The linebackers, when not assigned to predetermined stunts, like any other linebacker in the game of football, are expected to read and to react to their keys.

Obviously, attack defenses are reluctant to send their linebackers on every play. Were they to do so, they would inadvertently incorporate an element of predictability into their defensive game plan, which is contrary to everything they represent. Much of this continues, then, to be an advantage for a well-designed and flexible offensive program.

Much of our success depends on linebackers and secondary personnel reading backfield personnel and reacting within the framework of *our* strategies. One of football's truisms states that it's hard to fool a dummy. Well, we're the first to admit that football players aren't dummies. The game has come too far in the past several years to allow for that.

But there are some defenses that aren't coached as well as others. For the defense that doesn't read backfield keys, elements of misdirection and sequence are lost on them. But usually everything else works, so we don't worry about them too much. You and I both know that our toughest opponents are well coached and, on that basis, are subject to the planned influences of the offensive attack.

That's where our self-scouting format comes in. If defenses attacked the line of scrimmage randomly with no attempt to capitalize on offensive tendencies, then our attempts at self-scouting wouldn't make very much sense. Given the fact that our program employs attack-defense principles, we know that good defensive coaches do their homework.

Such is the case with the universities of Wisconsin and Notre Dame. Each school was kind enough to share a considerable amount of information regarding the strategies they use against attack defenses. Fortunately, much of what they do is consistent with the principles we have already discussed in the foregoing pages.

So, rather than reinvent the wheel in this chapter, we'll avoid mention of strategies that are identical to ours and focus instead on a couple things they do that will expand on the principles we have discussed already. Let's look first at the University of Notre Dame.

NOTRE DAME

George Kelly has been a coaching fixture at Notre Dame for more years than he cares to remember—although his memories are rich with All-Americans and National Championships. The embodiment of the Notre Dame mystique, Kelly started as a player and returned as a coach after coaching high school and at the universities of Marquette and Nebraska, where he worked with and learned from such football legends as Lisle Blackburn and Bob Devaney.

During his long and successful tenure at Notre Dame, he has contributed to a brilliantly triumphant program, having worked with such established genuises as Dan Devine and Ara Parseghian. George Kelly knows his football. So let's borrow for a minute from his years of experience and see what Notre Dame does. Because George was one of my coaches at the University of Nebraska and has been a long-time friend, I have always been able to count on him for help.

THE PLAY-ACTION COMPONENT AT NOTRE DAME

Aside from recommending that we "Trap 'Em," George suggested the effectiveness of play-action passes, one of which is illustrated in figure 13-1. Described within our terminology, the play would be designated an "I 10/Naked bootleg at 7."

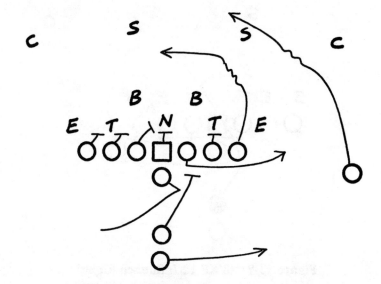

Figure 13-1 "I10/Naked bootleg at 7"

Obviously, the play capitalizes on the keys employed by a well-coached defense and utilizes an onside down-blocking scheme to prevent defensive penetration. Much of the play's success depends on the backfield faking and the pass-"deceiving" skills of both receivers.

The play also capitalizes on the principle that emphasizes using your tight end to find the areas of the defense vacated by the linebackers. Even if the linebackers aren't coming on predetermined stunts, they can't help but be influenced by the flow of the backfield and the movement of pulling guard.

Regarding the "Trap 'Em" principle, Notre Dame emphasizes two excellent plays versus the 6-1 and the split 6. The first, versus the 6-1 (or 4-3; call it what you want), utilizes imagination as well as solid common sense. Figure 13-2 illustrates the "I 8/Cross fire 12/ Influence Right."

Any good middle linebacker is likely to key the fullback *through* the center and two guards. His awareness of what the "triangle" is doing generally provides clues regarding the point of attack. This particular play of Notre Dame's provides such clues, but it confuses them with added offensive maneuvers that are inconsistent with the linebackers's usual keys.

For example, whenever the center blocks off, the middle linebacker normally fills behind him, expecting to jam the point of attack. That's precisely what he'd do in this case—were it not for the pulling guards and the tailback flying hard to the outside. Complicate his decision further by running the Cross fire option at 8 with the same blocking and

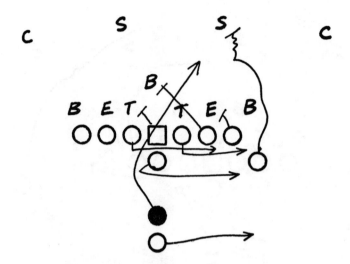

Figure 13-2 "I8/XF 12/Influence Right"

backfield scheme, only with a fullback fill, as in figure 13-3, and as the game progresses, the middle linebacker is going to get lost in the shuffle.

It's a well-conceived sequence and it not only complicates the middle linebackers's job but also provides the manpower along the line of scrimmage to prevent penetration from even the most zealous attack defense. So does the play in figure 13-4, an "I 8/Fullback Quick at 12 trap," illustrated versus a split 6.

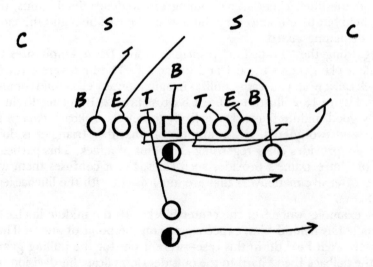

Figure 13-3 "I8/XF option at 8"

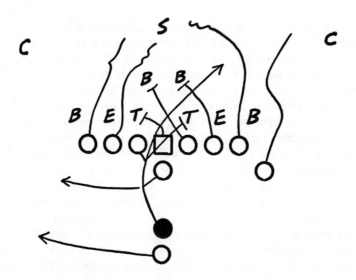

Figure 13-4 "I8/FB Quick at 12 T"

It's very similar to our own 12 trap, but it's described again in this chapter because Notre Dame indicates that defenses often blitz a strong safety to take away their power play at the off-tackle hole. These are times, obviously, when self-scouting comes in handy. This is the perfect time for Notre Dame—and for us—to show our I 8 formation and, during the appropriate down and distance, when the defense is expecting a power play, to run the quick at 12 trap up the gut. If it gets through the line of scrimmage—and it has every chance to do just that—there is no one in the secondary to stop it.

Notre Dame shared more plays, but the others are largely consistent with strategies we have described already in earlier chapters. So we thank Coach Kelly for his assistance, and we move on to the University of Wisconsin and to the help of Coach Fred Jackson.

THE UNIVERSITY OF WISCONSIN

Fred Jackson is just one of several assistant coaches at the University of Wisconsin who have been instrumental in helping head coach Dave MacClain realize the school's present level of football success. What was once the Big Two in the Midwest is becoming again the Big Ten, due largely to the efforts of fine coaches like Dave MacClain and Fred Jackson. The University of Wisconsin has reestablished itself as one of the finest football programs in the country. One of the reasons involves an intelligently conceived offensive attack.

The first question we asked Coach Jackson was "When preparing to play a team that uses an attack defense, what guiding principles do you keep in mind offensively?" We were pleased that his answers reaffirmed just about everything we have discussed to this point. Like Notre Dame, the University of Wisconsin likes to trap attack defenses.

They also emphasized the use of screen passes, particularly against defenses that blitz the strong safety and/or the weakside cornerback. Coach Jackson made particular mention of assuring wide line splits in order to run dive plays and to use backs as blockers, a strategy we have discussed extensively in earlier chapters. Finally, he suggested the use of misdirection to confuse linebacker and secondary keys.

We were pleased that each of Fred's suggestions was consistent with our principles, so let's look at one of their favorite plays, as illustrated in figure 13-5, a play that has proved to be one of the most consistently effective in *our* offensive attack. Using our terminology, it would be designated an "I 8/Power at 2," It capitalizes on the blocking talents of the fullback.

Recall from earlier chapters that a blocking back frees up one of the offensive linemen to help out with a double-team block at the point of attack. Against a five-man front, the strategy provides a particulary effective play. At the risk of beating a good idea to death, we'll repeat simply that the strategy absolutely neutralizes a slashing noseman, no matter how quick he is.

If he stunts *away* from the point of attack, we let him go. The onside guard simply plateaus to the offside linebacker, who may or may not be

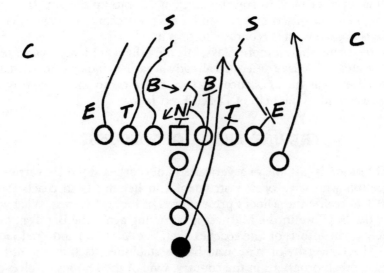

Figure 13-5 "I8/Power at 2 lead"

coming on a predetermined scrape with the noseman. If he stunts *into* the point of attack, he slants right into a double-team block. The lead back, in Wisconsin's case the fullback, goes right to the onside linebacker. If the linebacker scrapes himself away from the point of attack, the fullback continues toward the safety for a touchdown block.

As you already know, we like to run the play from a full house formation. We do it from a variety of other formations as well, but we particularly like the full house because it enables us to run the lead play from cross fire action. The fullback fake to the opposite side of the point of attack helps keep the offside linebacker honest. In addition, the fullhouse, being a balanced set, doesn't provide the obvious kinds of tendencies provided by other formations.

NOTHING NEW

Well, if you prize yourself on being a student of the game, your first lesson probably revealed the fact that nothing much in football is really *new*. Coaches, like standup comics, (hopefully the similarity ends there!) borrow unashamedly from each other. What flourished and was forgotten years ago is likely to be resurrected by some bright light who is either reinventing the wheel or rediscovering the worth of an old idea.

The use of backs as blockers is neither old nor new; it represents one of those constants that has become ingrained in many programs. We depend on it; so does Wisconsin. Their "I 8 Power at 2" is but one example. Consider figure 13-6 as another example.

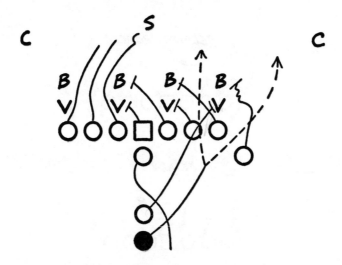

Figure 13-6 "I8/Power right"

We would call it an "I 8/Power right/Straight blocking" and, like Wisconsin, would enjoy running it against a 4-4 stack because of the angle blocks it provides along the line of scrimmage. The wingback's presence also creates that tenth gap along the line of scrimmage that is so troublesome to even an eight-man defensive front.

The fullback's inside-out block at the six hole completes the defense's dilemma. His responsibility is to block the man in the outside tandem who defends the inside area. The wingback is instructed to shield block the player in the tandem who comes to the outside. Obviously, the tailback has the option to run behind the fullback at six or outside the wingback at eight. That is why it is necessary to position him seven to eight yards deep in the backfield.

Again, we feel the need to emphasize a self-scouting format that provides a pretty good "guesstimate" of just the right time to run the play. Wisconsin identified three attack modes run out of the 5-2 that characterize the play of several of their opponents.

Illustrated in figure 13-7, the attack modes provide both confusion for the offense and a well-conceived pattern of stunts to blanket the line of scrimmage. They are not particularly complicated and reflect a "right-

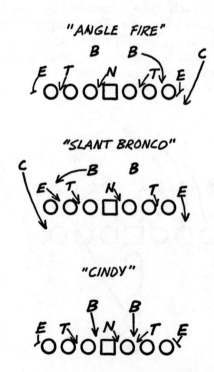

Figure 13-7 "Angle Fire" "slant bronco" "Cindy"

left" line slanting scheme employed by many teams using a five-man defensive front. The slants are sometimes executed randomly, but most often are called within the framework of the opponent's offensive tendencies.

The same is true of the "Cindy" call. Whereas the line slants may be called into or away from the strength of the formation depending on tendencies, they are designed to stop most any kind of play. The "Cindy" call is designed to jam the middle and, as such, may sacrifice some strength at the off-tackle holes. This represents yet another reason why self-scouting enables us to come closer to running the right play at the right time.

Assume, for example, that one of our pronounced tendencies in the I 7 formation is to run the deep power left. If we have scouted ourselves consistently and are aware of the tendency—or have *established* it for a big game—we can feel relatively confident that at some point in the game, the defense is going to execute the "Slant bronco" when we line up in an I 7.

It is at times like these that the offense wants to execute a screen play, as illustrated in figure 13-8, or run a lead play up the gut, or as diagrammed in figure 13-9, misdirect the defense with a counter play off deep power action. Each of the plays is very effective against this particular pattern of stunts, especially when a self-scouting format provides clues regarding the "when" and the "how" of their execution.

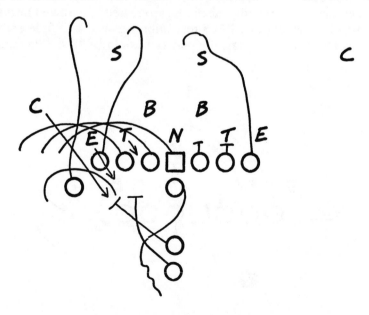

Figure 13-8 "I7/Power FB Screen left"

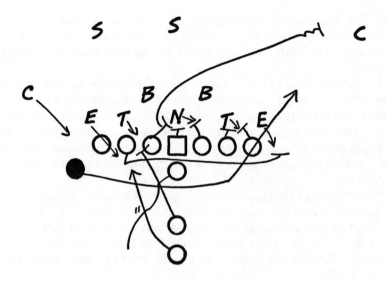

Figure 13-9 "I7/Power counter at 6"

EXPLOITING THE NINTH GAP

Wisconsin also recommended a principle we have described in an earlier chapter, namely, exploiting the ninth gap created by a winged formation. Figure 13-10 illustrates a Pro 8 formation versus a split 6 defense. According to our terminology, the play call would be "Pro 8/Power right/

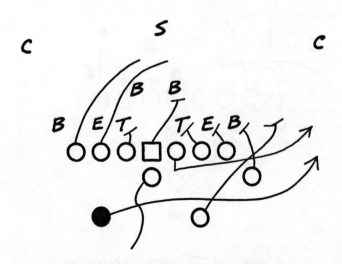

Figure 13-10 "Pro 8/Power right/Guard on"

Guard on" and would capitalize on the relatively weak containment capability of the split 6.

As evidenced in the diagram, the play provides for angle blocks at the point of attack and two lead blockers; the onside guard and the fullback. Obviously, the play is similar to the power play illustrated and discussed earlier in this chapter. Against the split 6, the play is committed to the outside because of the positioning of the defensive personnel.

Certainly, the defense can align itself somewhat differently, especially if the wingback does a number on the defensive end/outside backer. But if they do adjust their alignment, they are using a defense that they would prefer not to use. For example, if they put the strong safety closer to the off-tackle hole and adjust the end to the outside, we can consider play-action passes or a weakside attack. Any adjustment on their defense, particularly if it is unplanned, is another advantage for us.

TIME FACTORS

Clearly, most of the country's football programs don't enjoy the generous resources of a Notre Dame or a Wisconsin. To expect ourselves to achieve their level of sophistication in scouting procedure, personnel, and computer use is unreasonable. We can, however, incorporate a scouting *format* that is every bit as good as the ones they use. If we want to achieve a consistent level of success in our programs, it is necessary to adopt similar self-scouting concepts.

We may not have the resources available to us to determine the interrelationships among the variable levels of tendencies we have exhibited, but we can gain at least generalized understanding of what we *tend* to do during any given game. For programs with limited resources— and that includes most of us—our format is made to order. Even your team's manager, or one of the "walking wounded" from the previous week, can trail you on the sidelines writing down the plays as you call them.

If time is a factor—and it always is—borrow what we have discussed in the previous chapter and during much of this chapter. The concepts will introduce to you and your staff an added responsibility, but they will pay dividends far in excess of the added amount of time that will be required of you.

LET'S WRAP IT UP

First of all, our thanks to Coaches Kelly and Jackson for their contributions in this chapter. We are pleased that *their* principles against attack defenses are fundamentally the same as ours. The strategies we both employ have passed the test of time, for us and for them.

Let's not lose sight of the fact, however, that they are not guaranteed to work every time. To quote Bobby Burns again: "The best laid schemes of mice and men (and coaches!) often go astray." Sometimes we relax a bit too long and we get out-coached. Sometimes we don't do all our homework. On other occasions, as we've learned far too painfully, we get out-played. So the principles contained in this book aren't designed to work magic.

They are designed to emphasize ten or eleven important considerations to keep in mind when you are next preparing to play an attack defense. They are developed within the framework of several other basic assumptions: that you share the belief of all successful football coaches that the fundamentals of execution are the backbone of any effective offense, that consistently winning coaches are not afraid to burn the midnight oil doing their homework, and that the game of football is overflowing with great ideas just waiting for our perceptions to grow a little sharper to realize them.

It is to be hoped that we have provided a few ideas for your program. You must provide the work. But each of us learned a long time ago that nothing is work—unless you'd rather be doing something else. And I'll wager that neither one of us has found an alternative that even comes close to the fascination and the personal fulfillment of coaching football.

Index